Romantik
Journal for the Study of Romanticisms

Romanti*k*
Journal for the Study of Romanticisms

Volume 11|2022

V&R unipress

Contents

Introduction

When sending out the call-for-papers for the 11th issue of *Romantik – Journal for the Study of Romanticisms*, we decided to bring a painting by the Finnish painter Edvard Isto, *The Attack* from 1899. It depicts a double-headed eagle trying to clutch a law book from a young woman who heroically tries to defend herself against the predator. The background of this allegory was the unconstitutional Russification policies in Finland at the time. The eagle heraldically symbolizes Russia while the "Finnish Maiden" clutches the law book against the eagle's tearing grip. The choice of cover was, of course, not accidental. On February 24th 2022, Russia invaded Ukraine – showing that the tension between the Russian empire and neighbouring national states was not just a historical theme of late-romantic painting, but regrettably highly topical. In the current issue of *Romantik*, we bring an article by the Ukrainian scholar Inga Kapustian that gives the reader a part of the cultural background of the conflict between the former Soviet republic Ukraine and the culturally and politically dominating Russia. In her article "The Evolution of Ukrainian Literary Reception: Insights from Translation of Hans Christian Andersen's Works", Kapustian demonstrates that the translation history of Hans Christian Andersen in Ukraine reflected oppressive Russian/Soviet language politics. Furthermore, the spiritual aspects of Andersen's works were ideologically redefined to conform with official Soviet atheism.

One of the other main themes of the current issue of *Romantik* is the journey which – as a literary topos – is as old as literature itself: We just have to think of Homer's *Odyssey*, Swift's *Gulliver's Travels*, Tristam Shandy's *A Sentimental Journey*, etc. In the early 1800s, we see the theme culminating in romantic authors such as Ludwig Tieck (*Franz Sternbalds Wanderungen*), William Wordsworth (*The Prelude, The Excursion*), as well as in the period's famous travelogues by e.g. F-R. de Chateaubriand, Alphonse de Lamartine, or Hans Christian Andersen. The current issue of *Romantik* examines the historico-cultural potential in two influential authors of the romantic era: Lea Grosen Jørgensen treats the discovery journey to Vinland as a motif in Adam Oehlenschläger's saga play *Landet fundet og forsvundet* and Anders Kristian Strand studies the changing descriptions of the Scottish landscape around the river Yarrow in William Wordsworth's Yarrow poems. The geographical location as a catalyst for poetic fantasy is the subject of both places, the methodological approach that is used, however, shows something about the scope of current romantic studies: Oehlenschläger's Vinland play is read against the background of the period's critical reception of Icelandic sagas, e.g., as part of the period's philological and scientific history discourse while Wordsworth's Yarrow poems are interpreted in the perspective of personal creative memory and at the same time seen as part of a fashion of 'literary tourism' established in the early decades of the nineteenth century.

In this issue of *Romantik*, the two art historical contributions seek to place the artists and their artwork in a complex world of aesthetics, power, and politics: In Edward Payne's article, the Spanish baroque painter Jusepe de Ribera's (1591–1652) taste for violence is being nuanced and explained with reference to French romantic poetry while Hans Erik Havsteen analyzes the Danish neoclassical sculptor Bertel Thorvaldsen's (1770–1844) overlooked hidden political agency. These articles offer their readers a new understanding of the nature of romanticism and neoclassicism, especially the way both movements transgress a more conventional definition of their characteristics when societal and political changes are taken into account. As such, these contributions are in accordance with the original intent of *Romantik* since its very beginning: a constant examination of the concept of romanticism.

By thematizing what he calls 'artistry' versus 'artifice', Edward Payne introduces a romantic French nineteenth-century poet's reception of a Spanish seventeenth-century baroque painter and, thus, makes ideas of romanticism accessible as studies of visuality and poetic responses in times of political unrest. As his starting point, Payne takes Théophile Gautier's (1811–1872) reception of a selection of Ribera's most violent and complex depictions of mythological sinners (Tityus and Ixion) and unfolds layers of punishment, bodily unmaking, iconography, and spectatorship. Payne seeks to understand the duality in Ribera by focusing on his different artistic roles as both a painter of bodily pain and a creator of torture, and by stressing this duality he establishes a more nuanced view of the artist and the series of Fallen Giants.

Hans Erik Havsteen explores how Thorvaldsen can be perceived as a political artist through his work on the Alexander Frieze which was commissioned to celebrate Napoleon's (later cancelled) visit to Rome in 1812. Havsteen argues that the political aspects of Thorvaldsen's art have been neglected due to a one-sided understanding of neoclassical art as well as a dominating nationalistic interpretation of the sculptor. A closer reading of the source material shows how Thorvaldsen made room for a far more critical representation of the French emperor which contrasts with the widespread notion that the cosmopolitan artist refrained from expressing any political opinions. The study underlines how subtle opposing messages had to be expressed in Thorvaldsen's work. Furthermore, by examining the reception history of the Alexander Frieze, the author unfolds how Thorvaldsen's interest in the Greek style of antiquity (instead of the Roman) places him in the German liberal circles of Friedrich Schiller and the Humboldts who also strongly opposed the French regime.

Welcome to the 11th issue of *Romantik*.

Gísli Magnússon, Marie-Louise Svane, and Sine Krogh,
on behalf of the editorial board

Inga Kapustian
(University of Southern Denmark)

The Evolution of Ukrainian Literary Reception: Insights from the Translation of Hans Christian Andersen's Works

Abstract
This article examines the reception of Hans Christian Andersen's tales in Ukraine by analyzing the translation history, socio-political context, and cultural interpretation. It explores the complex ways in which the understanding of translation has changed as it was influenced by Ukraine's relationship with Russia and the Soviet Union and the impact of these factors on dissemination and interpretation. The study also investigates the cultural comprehension of Andersen's works in Ukraine, focusing on translating Christian motifs and reflecting Ukrainian cultural perspectives on religion. Additionally, it considers the influence of Soviet-era translation censorship on the reception and interpretation of Andersen's tales. By connecting these objectives, the article provides insights into the role of Andersen's tales in Ukrainian literature and society, highlighting the historical context, societal values, and challenges faced during the translation process. The study contributes to a deeper understanding of the reception and interpretation of Andersen's tales within the Ukrainian literary landscape.

Keywords
Hans Christian Andersen, Ukrainian interpretation, Christian motifs, Soviet values, cultural perspective

Introduction

The understanding of the reception of Hans Christian Andersen's literary works in Ukraine should be approached by exploring its translation history, socio-political context, and the cultural interpretation of his tales. The translation history of Andersen's works in Ukraine has been complex and heavily influenced by Ukraine's social and political history, particularly its relationship with Russia and the Soviet Union. The article will examine the impact of these factors on the dissemination and interpretation of Andersen's tales in Ukraine.

Additionally, the investigation of the cultural comprehension of Andersen's works in Ukraine will yield valuable insights into the manner and structure in which his tales have been received and interpreted by Ukrainian readers. A particular aspect of interest pertains to the translation of Christian motifs found within Andersen's tales, elucidating their reflection of wider cultural perspectives on religion and spirituality within Ukraine.

By connecting these *objectives*, the article aims to provide a comprehensive understanding of the role of Andersen's tales in Ukrainian literature and society, as well as the factors that have influenced their reception and interpretation. In this context, especially the impact of Soviet-era translation censorship on the reception and interpretation of Andersen's tales in Ukrainian literature and society. The article seeks to uncover the nuances that influenced the understanding and perception of Andersen's tales within Ukrainian literature by examining the societal values, beliefs, and norms that prevailed during the time of translation.

Exploring the Historical Context of the Translation of Andersen's Tales in Ukraine

The literary landscape in Ukraine has undergone a major transformation in recent years, with a renewed emphasis on understanding how historical and social factors have influenced the interpretation of literary works that have been translated from foreign languages into native languages.[1] The translation history of Andersen's tales in Ukraine is a complex and fascinating study area, with a rich cultural heritage dating back to the 19th century when the promotion of Ukrainian translations began. To understand the current state of the problem, it is important to consider its historical context and theoretical issues of Ukrainian *translatology* as a science. Throughout history, including periods of censorship, repression, and Russification, Ukrainian society, and its literary system faced various challenges.

The study by Shmiher is of particular interest in connection with a social understanding of Hans Christian Andersen's tales that have been influenced by cultural, political, and national upheavals in Ukrainian society, first in the context of the Russian Empire and later in the Soviet Union. Shmiher writes:

> The most crucial aspect in the history of translation studies is its periodization. The development of internal regularities, as well as the influence of other scientific paradigms from various traditions and disciplines, and socio-political factors such as dominant ideologies and socio-economic features, directly shape the distinct stages of this

1 Taras Shmiher, *Istoriia ukrainskoho perekladoznavstva KhKh storichchia: kliuchovi problemy ta periodyzatsiia [The History of Ukrainian Studies of the 20th Century: Key Issues and Periodization]* (Kyiv: Smoloskyp, 2008).

> field. These factors contribute to the accumulation of information and the deepening of analytical tools in translation studies.[2]

Particularly, the study highlights the impact of these transformations on artistic translation as a cultural phenomenon which has been shaped by the rich and complex Ukrainian reality.

One significant event in the history of Ukrainian literature that exemplifies these influences is the issuance of the *Valuev circular* in 1863. In his research, Johannes Remy shed light on the significant impact of language restrictions on the Ukrainian population during the period he examined.[3] The regulation limited the printing of many publications (religious, educational) and literature recommended for use in primary literacy training of the people and other works in the Ukrainian language. Remi admitted that the official imperial position was that the Ukrainian language did not exist, and that what existed was, at most, a dialect. Often, Ukrainian national activists played by the government's rules, calling Ukrainian (or Little Russian, or South Russian) a dialect. In most cases, this was a tactical choice to get their message through. Thus, the Ukrainian language was forbidden, except for works belonging to *belles-lettres*. The *circular* regulation claimed that this type of Ukrainian language was a form of dialect. The *Valuev circular* quoted the opinion of the Kiev Censorship Committee that Ukranian as a separate "Little Russian" (Malorosiia) language never existed, does not exist, and shall not exist, and their "Little Russian" mother tongue used by commoners is nothing but Russian corrupted by the influence of Poland. In his circular regarding Ukrainian publications, Valuev quoted opinions that denied the existence of the language and stated that the local dialect was nothing but Russian corrupted by Polish influence. The Ukrainian language, commonly referred to as 'Petit-russien' (Malorossijskii), witnessed an interesting linguistic phenomenon in the translation of Hans Christian Andersen's story "Mother" which was published in St. Petersburg in 1894 following the implementation of restrictive laws concerning the Ukrainian language.[4] When examining the translation of the story's title, *Historien om en Moder*, it is intriguing to observe that it was written in Russian letters as *Мать* but pronounced phonetically in Ukrainian ('Petit-russien') for that time period. The primary peculiarity lay in the spelling and the use of specific

2 Shmiher, *Istoriia*, page 24.

3 Johannes Remy, "The Valuev Circular and Censorship of Ukrainian Publications in the Russian Empire (1863–1876): Intention and Practice." *Canadian Slavonic Papers / Revue canadienne des slavistes 49, no. 1/2* (2007): 87–110. https://doi.org/10.1080/00085006.2007.11092432.

4 Hans Christian Andersen, *Une Mere conte de Hans Christian Andersen en vingt-deux langues [The Story of a Mother by Hans Christian Andersen in twenty-two Languages]*, (Saint Petersbourg: S.M. Nicolaieff, 1894), 13.

letters, showcasing the intricate interplay between languages and linguistic practices.

Further restrictions were placed on Ukrainian by the Ems Ukaz in 1876. Using the Ukrainian language in open print for a wide audience was completely prohibited. Ems Ukaz [Емський указ; Ems'kyi ukaz], was a secret decree of Emperor Alexander II of Russia, issued in 1876, banning the use of the Ukrainian language in print except for reprinting old documents. *The Ukaz* also forbade the import of Ukrainian publications and the staging of plays or lectures in Ukrainian.

During this period of Ukrainian translations of Hans Christian Andersen's works, the analysis task becomes challenging due to the involvement of the censors in the Russian editions. Although Anna Hansen (or Anna and Peter Hansen) is credited as the translator in the Russian editions, the censors changed the translations. Ukraine discovered the legacy of Hans Christian Andersen in 1873. Then, for the first time, 24 fairy tales by the Danish writer were published in Ukrainian, translated by M. Starytsky as "Andersen's Fairy Tales with a Short Biography". The works of Andersen were translated into Russian by the Ukrainian writer Marko Vovchok.[5] Regarding Marko Vovchok, it is worth mentioning the work, by Inna Sergienko, which highlights the role of the Ukrainian writer as a translator of *The Complete Fairy Tales of H.C. Andersen* during the 1850–60s. Sergienko mentioned the Ukrainian writer and translator among other Russian translators which could give us reason to suggest that Vovchok resorted to translating into Russian due to the restrictions imposed on the publication of works in Ukrainian, such as the Valuev circular and other regulations issued by Russia during that period. This creative translation approach allowed Vovchok to navigate the limitations and contribute to the dissemination of Andersen's fairy tales in a language accessible to a broader audience. Subsequently, Andersen was translated by P. Grabovskyi, M. Zahirnia (M. Grinchenko: 50 fairy tales, united under the name *Andersen's Tales*, 1906, 1918, 1919), Olena Pchilka, M. Rylskyi, and others. The collection *Princess on a Pea* (1956) and *Fairy Tales* (1964, 1970, 1977) were translated by Oksana Ivanenko. Andersen's works were also translated into Ukrainian by Yuriy Fedkovich, Maria Grinchenko, Agatangel Krymskyi, Halyna Kyrpa, Olga Senyuk, and others.

Beginning in the pre-revolutionary period, Hans Christian Andersen's authorship was translated by M. Starychenko (later name Starytskyi) and published in Kyiv in 1873. Since that time, and later in the Soviet and post-Soviet periods, scholars translated fairy tales of Andersen from Russian and English into Ukrainian. This genealogy and complex web of intermingling sources and target languages – as well as cultures – can be considered as a background for un-

5 Marina Balina, Mads Sohl Jessen, Ben Hellman, and Johs Frandsen, *Hans Christian Andersen in Russia* (Odense: University Press of Southern Denmark, 2020).

derstanding the peculiarities of translation studies. Mykhailo Starytskyi was the first translator of some of Andersen's tales. Over the course of his life, he worked as a writer, translator, and playwright but all these activities were involved with the establishment of new Ukrainian literature.[6] Starytskyi began his poetic work with translations of Alexander Pushkin, Mikhail Lermontov, Mykola Nekrasov, Heinrich Heine, George Byron, Adam Mickiewicz, Serbian songs, etc.

The book of fairy tales, translated and published by Starytskyi, was called "Andersen's Tales with a Short Biography". This edition was unique regarding its translation and illustrations. The biography of Hans Christian Andersen and 11 drawings were added to the fairy tales, the collection contains 24 fairy tales, comprising 362 pages, and was printed in Kyiv in 1873.

Unveiling the Reception and Adaptation of Andersen's Tales in Ukraine: Censorship, Ideology, and Acculturation in Translation

In February 1918, the Council of People's Commissars of Soviet Russia issued the Decree on Separation of Church from State and School from Church which stripped religious organizations of their property and legal status. This move paved the way for promoting atheistic propaganda and education to eliminate religion and replace it with a materialistic world view. The anti-religious campaign that lasted from 1921 to 1941 formed the basis of the USSR's efforts to eradicate religion, resulting in the closure of thousands of churches and the execution of thousands of priests. The Russian Orthodox Church was considered part of the previous political and ideological system and, therefore, had to be eradicated. In the literary domain, censorship extended to all references to religion, God, and the Bible, both in re-editions of old books and new books.

The state's censorship of printed materials in the Soviet Union was the responsibility of the Main Directorate for Literary and Publishing Affairs, commonly referred to as Glavlit (abbreviation of Main Directorate for Literary and Publishing Affairs), established in 1922 and operational until 1991 under different names.[7]

The severity of censorship depended on the shifting political climate and agenda. Therefore, the censorship of Andersen's translations depended on the state's current stance on religion and ideological beliefs. As a result, the texts underwent changes that could alter their meaning and, consequently, the read-

6 Natalia Mykolaivna Piven, "Mykhailo Starytskyi: Shliakh do Poezii cherez poetychni pereklady", [Mykhailo Starytskyi: The Path to Poetry through Poetic Translations], *Contemporary Challenges and Current Problems of Science, Education, and Production* (Kyiv, 2021): p. 369.

7 Leonid Vladimirov "Glavlit: How the Soviet Censor Works", *Index on Censorship 1, no. 3–4* (1972), 31–43. https://doi.org/10.1177/030642207200103-404.

er's interpretation. The selection of works to translate was heavily influenced by Soviet doctrines. During the 1930s and beyond, when Zerov was working as a translator, a special department regulated the list of artistic works that could be translated and popularized. This regulation dictated which foreign authors could be translated and what works were considered acceptable for translation. In one of these documents, edited in 1930 (*"скандинавська література"*, Scandinavian Literature), there was a permit for translation of Scandinavian literature.[8]

This was the background for including and censoring Andersen's fairy tales. The norm of Soviet doctrines thus played a significant role in determining the scope and direction of translation activity during this period. The impact of repression was significant in the field of Ukrainian translation studies during the second half of the 1930s and the first half of the 1940s, particularly during the wartime period. Most scientific articles during this time were obligated to include Stalinist rhetoric which persisted until the mid-1950s.[9] During this era, a substantial transformation took place regarding the theoretical foundations of study and criticism, as well as the activities of academic journals and the views of researchers regarding the Marxist methodology and ultimately resulted in a significant decrease in critical publications.

Andersen's reception in Ukraine, as a country that was historically part of the Russian Empire and later became a member of the Soviet Union, unveils two intriguing mechanisms of reception.[10] On the one hand, the scholars and literates responsible for introducing Andersen's works to Ukrainian readers often undertook modifications in the translations with the aim of infusing them with a pedagogical, moral, or nationalistic tendency. These alterations served the purpose of aligning Andersen's tales with the specific educational, moral, and cultural goals within a Ukrainian context. Whilst the majority of translations remained faithful to the underlying content of Andersen's works, the Ukrainian environment exerted its influence on the adaptation of the stories, shaping them to resonate with the socio-political climate and cultural values of the time.[11] This process of acculturation, where the original texts were subtly transformed to better suit the local context, represents a recurrent phenomenon observed in the translation literature of the discussed time period.

8 Shmiher, *Istoriia*, 303.

9 Sheila Fitzpatrick "Culture and Politics under Stalin: A Reappraisal." *Slavic Review 35, no.* 2 (1976), 211–231. https://doi.org/10.2307/2494589.

10 Oleksandr Kal'nychenko, "A Sketch of the Ukrainian History of Translation of the 1920s." in *Between Cultures and Texts: Itineraries in Translation History*, ed. Antoine Chalvin, Anne Lange and Daniele Monticelli (Frankfurt am Main, P. Lang, 2011), 235–248.

11 Vitaly Chernetsky "Nation and translation." In *Contexts, Subtexts and Pretexts*, ed. Brian J. Baer (Kent: John Benjamins Publishing Company, 2011), 2.

For instance, prominent works such as "The Snow Queen", "Ole Lukoie" and "The Little Mermaid" suffered from various omissions that were indicative of the prevailing ideological and cultural climate. Numerous passages were deliberately excluded, resulting in significant alterations of the original text. These omissions primarily targeted the removal of religious references, as they were deemed incompatible with the atheistic principles and ideological stance of the Soviet regime. The censors, driven by the objective of purging any associations with religion, sought to eradicate all mentions of God, the church, or other religious institutions from the translated versions of Andersen's tales. Consequently, the translated works underwent a transformation that aligned them with the prevailing ideological framework, thus serving to reinforce the desired narrative and cultural norms of the time. As a result, critical publications experienced a notable decline in frequency and scope.

In the article's frame, particularly considering the impact of Soviet-era translation censorship on the reception and interpretation of Andersen's tales in Ukrainian literature and society, two intriguing reception mechanisms come to light. On the one hand, scholars and literates who introduced Andersen to Ukrainian readers often modified the translations to have a pedagogical, moral, or nationalistic bent. Although most of the translations remained faithful to Andersen's content, in some cases, the Ukrainian environment influenced the adaptation of the stories. This kind of acculturation is common in the translation literature of the time discussed.

For example, 'The Snow Queen,' 'Ole Lukoie,' and 'The Little Mermaid' suffered from various omissions that were typical of the period. Many passages were deleted, resulting in significant changes to the original text. The censors' primary goal was to eliminate any reference to God, the church, or other religious institutions.[12]

To exemplify this, I analyze the changes made in the translation of religious motifs and themes such as 'the Lord', 'prayer', 'angels', 'pious', 'an immortal soul', 'Kingdom of God'. The Danish version of the fairy tales is taken from the 1992 edition of Hans Christian Andersens *Samlede Eventyr og Historier* and the Ukrainian translation done by Oksana Ivanenko during 1975–1977th.[13] These excerpts illustrate the changes in the translation from the source text to the target text and we may assume that the censors' primary goal was to eliminate any reference to God, the church, or other religious institutions.

---

12 Oleksandr Kalnychenko and Lada Kolomiyets. "Translation in Ukraine During the Stalinist Period: Literary Translation Policies and Practices." In *Translation Under Communism* ed. Christopher Rundle, Anne Lange and Daniele Monticelli (Cham: Springer International Publishing, 2022), 141–172.

13 Hans Christian Andersen, Vilhelm Pedersen, Lorenz Frølich, and Estrid Dal, *Samlede eventyr og historier* (København: Hans Reitzels Forlag, 1992).

The Lord

Danish: Nu ville de også flyve op mod *Himmelen* selv for at gøre nar af englene og *"Vorherre".*

English: Now they wanted to fly up **to Heaven** itself to make fun of the angels and the 'Good Lord'.]

Ukranian: Тоді … захотіли полетіти **на небо** і там повеселитися. ("Snow queen" gloss text: Then….(they)….. wanted to fly **to the sky** and have fun there)

Analyzing the provided translation, it could be claimed that it reveals a deliberate omission of religious references, particularly in the case of "The Lord". In the original Danish version, the passage mentions flying up to Heaven to the angels and the "Good Lord". However, in the Ukrainian translation, the reference to the 'Good Lord' is entirely removed, and the focus shifts to simply wanting to fly to the sky and have fun there.

This alteration strongly suggests the influence of the censors' goal to eliminate any reference to God, the church, or other religious institutions. By removing the mention of the 'Good Lord', the translation veers away from religious connotations and aligns with the ideology of the ruling regime which sought to suppress religious beliefs and replace them with secular values.

The deliberate omission of religious references in the translation reflects the broader censorship policy of erasing religious elements from literary works. It demonstrates a systematic effort to reshape narratives and eliminate religious connotations that were deemed incompatible with Soviet ideology. This alteration impacts the overall interpretation of the tale by obliterating its spiritual dimensions and highlighting secular themes.

The Christ Child

Danish: Og de små holdt hinanden i hænderne, kyssede roserne og så ind i **Guds klare solskin** og talte til det, som om **Jesusbarnet** var der.

English: The children held each other by the hand, kissed the roses, looked up at the **God's clear sunshine**, and spoke to it as if the **Christ Child** were there.

Ukrainian: Діти тримали одне одного за руки, цілували троянду, дивилися на **сонечко** і розмовляли з ним. (Gloss text: The kids were holding each other's hands, kissing the roses, looking up **at the sun**, and talking to it). As we see from this part of the translated text the name of 'Christ' and 'God' were omitted and replaced by the concept of nature.

From the perspective of translation theory and the ideology of the Soviet regime, the translation of the concept of Christ in "The Christ Child" exhibits both omission and adaptation. The original Danish version depicts the children holding hands, kissing the roses, looking up at the Lord's clear sunshine, and speaking to it as if the Christ Child were present. However, in the Ukrainian translation, the concept of Christ is entirely omitted. The focus shifts to the woman singing to the boy, their mutual singing, the children holding hands, kissing the roses, looking at the sun, and engaging in conversation with it. The emphasis is placed on the beauty of the summer days and the enjoyment of sitting under the aromatic rose bushes which are portrayed as eternal and never fading. The religious symbolism and spiritual undertones of the original text are substituted with a focus on nature and the joys of earthly existence.

This adaptation demonstrates the power dynamics between translation and ideology. The translation serves as a tool for reshaping the narrative according to the prevailing ideology, stripping it of its religious connotations and replacing them with secular themes.

In terms of translation theory, this case exemplifies the complex relationship between the source text, the target culture, and the translator's agency. The translator, Oksana Ivanenko, likely had to navigate the constraints imposed by the censorship policy while maintaining some semblance of the original narrative.[14] However, the omission of Christ highlights the limitations and challenges translators face operating within a regime that strictly controlled the dissemination of religious ideas.

Previous studies conducted by Ukrainian scholars, such as Shmihers, Kochurs and Kolomiets have shed light on the significance of exploring original religious motifs and their removal in fairy tales. Analyzing the impact of these omissions can provide valuable insights into the thematic significance of these motifs and their absence on the overall narrative structure and interpretation of the tales. Moreover, the censorship of religious references in fairy tales raises profound questions about the preservation of cultural heritage and the transmission of values through storytelling.

14 Snizhana Zhygun "Creating Social Reality by Soviet Children's Publishing Companies in Ukraine in the 1920s and 1930s." *Libri & Liberi: časopis za istraživanje dječje književnosti i kulture* 11, no. 01 (2022), 35–50. https://doi.org/10.21066/carcl.libri.11.1.2.

The Lord's Prayer

Danish: Han var ganske forskrækket, han ville læse sit fadervor, men han kunne kun huske den store tabel.

English: He was quite frightened and wanted to say his Lord's Prayer, but all he could remember was his multiplication table.

Ukranian: Кай весь тремтів, хотів гукнути на допомогу своїх батьків, але в голові у нього була лише одна таблиця множення. (Gloss text: Kay was shivering and wanted to call his parents for help, but in his head there was only his multiplication table).

In this excerpt of the text, it is clear that the religious motifs such as the Lord's Prayer were omitted in the translations to comply with the Soviet policies, the modified text replaces the religious reference with a more neutral theme, the multiplication table. These adaptations were done to ensure that the stories were in line with the ideology and beliefs promoted by the Soviet state at the time. The aim was to present a version of the fairy tale that was devoid of religious elements and could be perceived as more secular or compatible with the Soviet worldview. It's worth noting that such changes and adaptations were not unique to "The Snow Queen" but were common for many literary works during the Soviet period.

Angels

Danish: Alle drømmene kom igen flyvende ind, og da så de ud som Guds engle, og de trak en lille slæde, og på den sad Kay og nikkede…

English: All the dreams came flying in once more, and then they looked like God's angels, and they pulled a small sled, and on it sat Kay and nodded…

Ukranian: … Сни знову прилинули в опочивальню. Здавалося, вони везли на маленьких саночках Кая, який кивав Герді головою. (Gloss text: The dreams again clinging to the bedchamber. They seemed to be carrying Kay on a small sled and he was nodding to Gerda), in this part, the translation was not done so accurately, God's angels were omitted and consequently, the whole idea was replaced and simplified, the angels transformed into just a child's dreams during the night.

Occasionally, when a religious theme serves a necessary purpose within a passage and the removal of a single word is not feasible, the entire passage was omitted. The examples demonstrate that the editor neglected many of Andersen's philosophical insights, cultural items, and personal vision. The requirement for children's literature to be straightforward and easily understood also played a role. One question that arises is whether the changes and omissions during that period were made by the editors, translators, or censors. Unfortunately, a definitive answer is difficult to obtain due to limited access to the archive on the territory of Ukraine at the moment.

The changes observed in Hans Christian Andersen's texts during this period are closely intertwined with the history of self-censorship in the Soviet Union which necessitates further investigation into the treatment of Andersen's fairy tales.

The mass production of translations from the national literature of the USSR commenced with the aid of Russian as a mediator language. Previously, translations were conducted directly from the original text, but the emergence of 'the mass Soviet reader' necessitated a shift towards using Russian as a relay language for translation.[15] This approach facilitated the translation process and enabled the creation of numerous translated works for the masses to read. In essence, using Russian as an intermediary language helped meet the demand for translated literature among the general Soviet population. During the Soviet era, the translation of Christian and religious motifs in Andersen's fairy tales was marked by a deliberate reconfiguration of values. This was achieved through the substitution or omission of elements present in the source text. Simultaneously, these translations were shaped by linguistic and theoretical approaches prevalent in contemporary translation theory.

The translators employed a conscious strategy of altering the religious and Christian content found in Andersen's fairy tales to align with the ideological objectives of the Soviet regime. This involved replacing or removing elements that contradicted the prevailing socialist principles and values. Taras Shmiher claims that by doing so, the translators sought to establish a new set of values within the translated texts which supported the ideological framework of the Soviet system.

At the same time, the translations during this period were informed by the linguistic and theoretical advancements in translation theory that were prevalent at the time. Translators drew upon these approaches to navigate the challenges posed by the reconfiguration of values and to ensure the coherence and intelligibility of the translated texts. The linguistic and theoretical underpinnings provided translators with tools and frameworks to address issues of equivalence, adaptation, and cultural context in their translation choices.

From the late 1930s onwards, the official Soviet doctrine vehemently criticized translational 'literalism' and advocated for 'free' translation. However, it is important to note that these guidelines were primarily enforced for direct translations from Western literature. In contrast, translations from Russian into Ukrainian, as well as other national languages within the Soviet Union, were subject

15 James Von Geldern and Richard Stites *Mass Culture in Soviet Russia: Tales, Poems, Songs, Movies, Plays, and Folklore, 1917–1953* (Indiana: Indiana University Press, 1995).

to a strict policy of literalism, enforced by editors, censors, and critics. According to Kolomiets and Kalnychenko, socialist realism ideologies denounced *elitist* literalism in translation, perceiving it as a manifestation of *literary formalism.* This term was used as a negative label since prioritizing form over content was considered contrary to the principles of socialist realism. Subsequently, it even became associated with 'cosmopolitanism'.[16] However, in practice, a double standard prevailed.

On the one hand, in terms of Andersen's fairy tale translations, it is evident that the censorship and ideological modifications imposed on the original text of *The Snow Queen* were greatly aided by the application of the *creative* translation strategy.[17] On the other hand, the Soviet translation school established a solid theoretical foundation for translation, which was also employed in Ukraine as part of the Soviet Union. In this regard, it is important to acknowledge the contributions of prominent Soviet translators of Andersen's works in Ukraine.

From a historical perspective in the field of translation studies, the development of two distinct approaches in the theory of translation – linguistic and literary – became evident during the 1940s. The linguistic approach, in essence, gained recognition at this time as it coincided with the emergence of translation theory itself. Regarding the research within the history of Ukrainian translation studies, Volodymyr Mykolaiovych Derzhavin drew upon the views of Oleksandr O. Potebnya while Oleksander M. Finkel highlighted the birth of a new discipline within linguistics known as linguistic stylistics.[18] Both V. Derzhavin and Oleksander Finkel developed two fundamental approaches to literary translation: a native-language-centered focus, which Derzhavin terms as "analogical" translation, and a foreign-language-centered, or "homological" or alternatively referred to as stylization in translation. It gives a foundation to conclude that according to their theoretical view translation operates at the intersection of two languages, cultures, literary traditions, and poetics, it entails making a choice between two possibilities: one is to focus on fidelity to the original, encompassing its language, cultural context, and stylistic nuances, while the other is to prioritize the reader, their language, cultural background, and preferences.

A number of investigations done by the well-known Ukrainian literary scholar Roksolana Zorivchak have shown that even earlier, Ivan Ya. Franko had made contributions to the field of stylistics. It is, therefore, logical that the theory of

16 Matthew T. Witt "Book Review: Kwame Anthony Appiah Cosmopolitanism: Ethics in a world of strangers. New York: WW Norton & Company, 2006." *Administrative Theory & Praxis* 28, no. 4 (2006), 646–652. https://doi.org/10.1080/10841806.2006.11029555.

17 E. G. Etkind "Creative Translation: Art and Science." *Soviet Studies in Literature 7, no. 3 (*1971): 171–195. https://doi.org/10.2753/RSL1061-19750703171.

18 L. M. Chernovatiy, *O.Finkel – Zabutyi teoretyk ukrayinskoho perekladoznavstva* [O. Finkel – the forgotten theoretician of Ukrainian translation studies] (Monohrafiya: Nova Knyha, 2007).

translation comprises two components – orientation towards the language system (or systems) and orientation towards the literary work system.[19] Consequently, two approaches have always coexisted within translation discourse – the distinction primarily lying in the emphasis on one of the two. However, the rapid advancement of linguistics – particularly the system theory of language and lexicography – significantly contributed to the increasing presence of linguistic topics in translation studies from the mid-20th century onwards.

Linguistic challenges in Ukrainian translation history

During the post-war decade, the spectrum of linguistic problems primarily revolved around Marxist-Leninist-Stalinist issues.[20] Researchers extensively analyzed translations of works in accordance with communist ideology, often highlighting the convergence of the Ukrainian and Russian languages. This convergence was occasionally achieved through interventionist methods. For instance, Oleksandr Biletskyi, the author, editor and compiler of anthologies on Russian, Ukrainian and foreign literature, editor of translations of world classics into Ukrainian, vehemently criticized the mechanical translation of Russian foreign words into Ukrainian which essentially turned the Russian-language dictionary into a Ukrainian one. Biletskyi questioned the scientific justification behind such phenomena and emphasized that "poetic vividness is not merely about expressing emotions in a straightforward manner. Rather, it involves a process of translating feelings into other poetic forms, the simpler this feeling is experienced, the more difficult its verbal expression is".[21] In his critique, Biletskyi raised significant questions regarding the scientific justification behind such phenomena and emphasized that poetic clarity in translation is best achieved by conveying feelings through creative transformation rather than resorting to direct expression. He argued that the simplicity of experienced emotions often makes their verbal expression more challenging. This perspective invites us to consider the importance of maintaining the delicate balance between linguistic accuracy and the artistic essence of translated works.

Many famous Ukrainian researchers studied theoretical translational phenomena and this article will draw attention to one of them. Taras Shmiher, who

19 Roksolana Zorivchak, "Patron Lvivskoho Universytetu yak zasnovnyk perekladoznavstva v Ukraini" [Lviv University Patron as Translation Studies Founder in Ukraine], *Visnyk Lviv University. Historical Series* 49 (2013): 319–327.

20 P.Y, Shalia and I. Horetskyi, *Ukraiinska mova: Praktycno-teoretychnyi kurs* [Ukrainian Language: Practical-and-Theoretical Course] (Kyiv: Knyhospilka, 1929).

21 Aleksandr Ivanovich Beletskiy, *V masterskoi khudozhnika slova* [In the artist's workshop] M.: Vyshaja shkola no. 2 (1989): 91.

suggests the periodization of the Ukrainian translations in the 1900s, argues that Ukrainian translation studies can be divided into four periods, namely the critical and theoretical period (1905–1920), the period of translation as an academic subject in Ukrainian research (1920–1945), Ukrainian Translation Studies within the context of the Soviet Union (late 1940 s – early 1970s), and the transformation into an interdisciplinary angle of research discourse (1970s till present), expanding the methods and areas of research involving developments in psycholinguistics, sociolinguistics, ethnolinguistics, and cultural studies.

The relationship between the state and literature is deeply intertwined, with language acting as a powerful tool through which the state establishes and reinforces its power. Literature becomes a vehicle for expressing and disseminating the state's preferred narratives, promoting cultural and national identity, and shaping public opinion. Looking at this from a modern vantage point, we could admit that the study of Pascal Casanova is very particular with regard to the concept of a national foundation of literature. The scientist admits in "Literature, Nation, and Politics": The link between the state and literature depends on the fact that, through language, the one serves to establish and reinforce the other.[22] These theoretical ideas created a background for understanding the reason why translation into the Ukrainian language was very complicated and diverse. Additionally, the state's control over literature through censorship and regulation further solidifies its influence over the literary realm. By considering these ideas regarding the translation of literary text with a 'domestication' approach to the source text, Ukrainian scholar Ilko Korunets' claims that "domestication is the means to enrich national languages and cultures, domestication (partly or complete) was and is the integral phenomenon in the historical development of the national language".[23]

During the 19th and early 20th centuries, literary translations played a significant role in the development of Ukrainian language and literature, as they were officially banned by the tsarist government. These translations, which included works by renowned writers like Ivan Franko, Marko Vovchok, Pavlo Grabovskyi, and Mykhailo Starytskyi, not only enriched the Ukrainian cultural context but also introduced new literary genres, such as sonnets and classical tragedy which were previously absent from Ukrainian discourse. Additionally, some translations into Russian, such as those of Jules Verne by Vovchok and Taras Shevchenko by Grabovskyi, contributed to the development of Ukrainian literary translation. Despite the 19th-century trend towards the Ukrainization of

22 Pascale Casanova, "Literature, Nation, and Politics." in *The Princeton Sourcebook in Comparative Literature: From the European Enlightenment to the Global Present* ed. Damrosch, David, Natalie Melas, and Mbongiseni Buthelezi, (Princeton: Princeton University Press, 2009): 329–41.

23 Ilko, V. Korunets, *Theory and Practice of Translation* (Vinnytsia: Nova Knyga, 2000).

translated literature, artistic translation in Ukraine served as a tool for nation-building, particularly in the face of official prohibitions, and continued to fulfil this role until Ukrainian independence was achieved. Hryhoriy Kochur, a renowned cultural studies scholar and skilled translator who worked with 33 different kinds of literature, proposed dividing the history of Ukrainian translation into distinct periods.[24] In the post-1917 era, Kochur identified two contrasting phases. The first 15 years after the revolution (up to 1932) were marked by great enthusiasm and a surge in translation activities. During this time, hundreds of translations were published from many different languages, along with multi-volume collections of translated authors. This period also saw a significant development in translation theory. The subsequent phase, from 1933 to the mid-1950s, witnessed a decline in translation activities, with numerous re-translations and relay translations typically made from Russian as the intermediary language.

It became common in the late 1930s for the names of recently repressed translators to be removed from newly published translations and many reprinted editions. Forewords and editorial notes, which were still acceptable, gradually became instruments for shaping the world view of 'an average Soviet reader' through abridgements and simplifications of the source text. Editors and translators were expected to work for a mass audience, especially for the cult of 'revolutionary' writers and members of the Communist Party. Consequently, a significant number of multi-volume projects that had been initiated earlier remained unfinished by the mid-1930s, and most manuscripts that had been prepared for publication were never published.

The literary policy of the later Soviet period was significantly influenced by changes in the country's political climate and a growing interest in foreign literature. In the years leading up to the Great Terror of 1937–38, which followed a decade of Cultural Renaissance, there was a significant decline in the number and quality of translations. Russian became the primary intermediary language, and in the 1950s, relay translation became mandatory in social sciences, allowing translations only from authorized Russian versions. The highest priority was given to contemporary Russian authors, followed by works by other Soviet writers of which the majority was translated from Russian as an intermediary or relay language. This approach became standard practice, while direct translations from other languages of the USSR were not as common.[25]

24 Lesia Kondratiuk, "Paraleli v zhytti ta tvorchosti M. Zerova ta H. Kochura" [Parallels In Life and Work of M. Zerov and H. Kochur] (*Visnyk Taras Shevchenko National University of Kyiv.* no 53, issue 1 (2021): 23–29.

25 L. Kolomiyets, "The Politics of Literal Translation in Soviet Ukraine: The Case of Gogol's "The Tale of How Ivan Ivanovich Quarreled with Ivan Nikiforovich"." *Translation and Interpreting Studies* no. 1 (2022).

Thus, according to Lyudmila Braude, in 1968 about 30 million copies of Andersen's works had been published. During the jubilee year, 1955, 120 thousand of his books came to the readers.[26] Lyudmila Braude, a famous researcher, reflected the idea which was very much cited and incorporated into the critical discourse about Andersen during the Soviet time. She claimed that Andersen teaches people that "the bright good faith will help to gain the victory of the sun over darkness, and a kind human heart over evil", and Hans Christian Andersen gained the second Motherland in our country (i. e. the Soviet Union).

To conclude, Ukrainian translation studies can be divided into four distinct periods, each characterized by different approaches and contexts: the critical and theoretical period, the period of translation as an academic subject in Ukrainian research, Ukrainian Translation Studies within the context of the Soviet Union, and the transformation into an interdisciplinary angle of research discourse. This periodization provides a framework for understanding the historical development and evolution of Ukrainian translation studies. Domestication, the approach of adapting a source text to enrich national languages and cultures, played a significant role in the translation of literary texts in Ukraine. It was viewed as an integral phenomenon in the historical development of the Ukrainian language. Hans Christian Andersen's literary works enjoyed substantial popularity in the Soviet Union, as indicated by the extensive publication of his works, as documented in Lyudmila Braude's article. Translations by Starytskyi and numerous other translators, both preceding the 1917 revolution and throughout the subsequent Soviet era, contributed to their wide dissemination. Notably, Oksana Ivanenko emphasized the presence of commendable moral lessons in Andersen's works and underscored his significant influence on critical discourse during the Soviet era, despite the deliberate removal and modification of religious symbols found in the original texts.

These conclusions shed light on the complex dynamics of the translation process in Ukraine and particularly Hans Christian Andersen's tales within this context, the historical settings of translation practices, and the impact of political and cultural factors on translation activities during the studied periods. Overall, the article suggests that translation is not a neutral or objective process but is shaped by the cultural, social, and political factors of the time and place in which it occurs.

26 Lyudmila Yulyevna Braude. *Zhyzn i tvorchestvo Khansa Khrystiana Andersena,* [Life and work of Hans Christian Andersen] (Leningrad, 1974).

Lea Grosen Jørgensen
(Aarhus University)

Remembering Norse America and Scandinavian Identity: Oehlenschläger's Heroic Vinland Play*

Abstract
This article analyzes Adam Oehlenschläger's *Landet fundet og forsvundet* (1846), a play mostly forgotten in Danish literary history. Taking the Vinland Sagas' narrative into consideration Oehlenschläger incorporates contemporary theories about the Norse discovery of America. With a special focus on the play's ending and main character Biørn Asbrandson, whom Oehlenschläger models after the Icelander of the same name in *Eyrbyggja Saga*, the article argues that the central theme of memory is displayed in a metatextual fashion: Through Biørn's lines, Oehlenschläger addresses his concern for Scandinavian identity and heritage in the light of rising emigration to America. Simultaneously, Biørn the Skald demonstrates how Oehlenschläger interprets the poet as a curator of memory, thus revealing the author's considerations about his own artistic legacy.

Keywords
Sagas, reception, medievalism, cultural memory, metatextuality

In Paris 1845, only five years before his death, Adam Oehlenschläger wrote the concise two-act-play *Landet fundet og forsvundet* (The Land found and lost, 1846). It was published in December 1845 and performed seven times at the Royal Danish Theatre, from May 17th, 1846, to November 23rd the same year. The first act was later rewritten posthumously as an opera with the new title *De to Armringe* (The two Arm Rings) and had likewise seven performances, this time from 1864 to 1866.[1]

Although *Landet fundet og forsvundet* has been overlooked in Oehlenschläger studies and Danish literary history in general, it is, like many of his famous

* Parts of the article are based on chapter 2.3. from the PhD thesis *Skjalde og skjaldskab: En komparativ analyse af den norrøne skjald hos Adam Oehlenschläger og N.F. S. Grundtvig* (Skalds and skaldic poetry: A comparative analysis of the Old Norse skald in Adam Oehlenschläger's and N.F.S. Grundtvig's authorships, 2020) by Lea Grosen Jørgensen. All English translations are my own.

1 F. L. Liebenberg, *Bidrag til den oehlenschlägerske Literaturs Historie. Andet Bind* (Copenhagen: J. H. Schultz, 1868), 363.

works, based on Old Norse literature and celebrates medieval Scandinavia. Specifically, the play is inspired by the Vinland voyages led by the Norseman Leif Erikson, also known as 'Leif the Lucky', son of Erik the Red. Around the year 1000, Leif established a settlement in a land west of Greenland, which he named Markland, Helluland, and Vinland; these areas have later been identified as North America. While Vinland is mentioned in medieval chronicles and Icelandic annals, the most notable and detailed descriptions of the voyages are found in the two sagas, *Eiríks saga rauða* (*Saga of Erik the Red*) and *Grænlendinga saga* (*Saga of the Greenlanders*), also commonly known as the Vinland Sagas.[2]

Eiríks saga rauða is preserved in the two manuscripts *Hauksbók* and *Skálholtsbók* which are presumed to date from the 14th to the 15th century, respectively. The events of *Grænlendinga saga* are part of the version of the saga about Olaf Tryggvason in *Flateyjarbók*, a manuscript from the 14th century. The two sagas are thought to be independent narratives though they are most likely based on the same oral or written sources, as their narratives overlap:[3] *Eiríks saga rauða* tells of the outlawed Erik's discovery and settlement in Greenland, and later of his son Leif's accidental discovery of unknown shores west of Greenland. In *Grænlendinga saga*, a similar discovery is made by Bjarni Herjólfsson. After hearing about these sightings, Leif buys Bjarni's ship and later visits the strange lands with an expedition of Norsemen. These include Leif's sister Freydis, his brother Thorvald, and Thorfinn Karlsefni and his wife Gudrid, a former widow of Erik's second son Thorstein. The Norsemen trade and have fatal disputes with natives in Vinland called Skraelings, and both sagas end with Gudrid and Thorfinn Karlsefni moving to Iceland with their son Snorri, the first Norseman born in Vinland. Three bishops are named as descendants from this bloodline.

The parts of the sagas concerning Vinland were translated into Latin in post-medieval Europe. Notable works include Johan Peringskiöld's 1697-translation of *Heimskringla*, Thormod Torfæus' *Historia Vinlandiæ* (History of Vinland, 1705), Paul-Henri Mallet's *Introduction à l'Histoire de Dannemarc* (Introduction to the History of Denmark, 1755), Thomas Percy's *Northern Antiquities* (1770), and Johan Reinhold Forster's *Geschichte der Entdeckungen und Schiffahrten im*

---

2 Vinland was first mentioned in Adam of Bremen's *Gesta Hammaburgensis ecclesiae pontificum* (*Deeds of the Bishops of Hamburg*, c. 1075). An entry for the year 1121 in an Icelandic annal also mentions a bishop named Erik from Greenland, who left in search for Vinland but was never heard from again. The latest medieval source about the subject is from another Icelandic annal, which refers to Markland in the entry for 1347 (Geraldine Barnes, *Viking America: The First Millennium* (Cambridge: D. S. Brewer, 2001), xii–xiii).

3 Jón Karl Helgason, *Echoes of Valhalla: The Afterlife of the Eddas and Sagas* (Reaktion Books, 2017), 156. Helgason consequently refers to *Grænlendinga saga* as *Ólafs saga Tryggvasonar.* I have chosen to use *Grænlendinga saga*, as I have observed that most post-medieval translators and editors prefer this title, including those at Oehlenschläger's time.

Norden (*History of Discoveries and Voyages made in the North,* 1784). However, the first modern translation of the Vinland Sagas came with Carl Christian Rafn's pivotal work *Antiquitates Americanæ* (1837), which openly claims that Norsemen discovered America 500 years before Christopher Columbus. In the latter part of the 19th century and the beginning of the 20th, this 'Viking theory' about America's Norse origin fascinated amateur archaeologists and Scandinavian Americans, who incorporated the Vinland voyages into a new national narrative.

Scholars agree that *Antiquitates Americanæ* initiated Old Norse interest in North America and began the scholarly search for Vinland as a geographical place.[4] Consequently, this has led to a relatively dominant focus on the sagas' historicity. During the last decades, however, researchers have challenged this tendency by introducing a more comparative outlook. Studies from Jerold Frakes[5], and more recently Pernille Hermann[6] and Annette Lassen[7] have examined the Vinland Sagas in accordance with other medieval literature by analyzing their Eurocentrism, supernatural elements, literary topography, or pagan aspects. Others, like Geraldine Barnes[8] and Jón Karl Helgason[9], have focused more intensely on the Vinland Sagas' reception, particularly their impact on 19th century British and American nationalism and 20th century Viking films. This comparative turn has expanded the literary and historical context (both medieval and post-medieval) for the study of the Vinland Sagas. As Brian Regal writes, the focus on Vinland alone even risks being constricting, as these narratives are barely twenty pages in total, a footnote in the corpora of Old Norse and medieval literature.[10]

When Oehlenschläger wrote his Vinland play, the authenticity of the sagas was front and centre. He most likely owned *Antiquitates Americanæ* and, like

---

4 Barnes, *Viking America*, 36; Birgitta Linderoth Wallace & William W. Fitzhugh, "Stumbles and Pitfalls in the Search for Viking America" in *Vikings: The North Atlantic Saga*, eds. William E. Fitzhugh and Elisabeth I. Ward (Washington and London: Smithsonian Institution Press, 2000), 375; Brian Regal, *The Battle over America's Origin Story: Legends, Amateurs, and Professional Historiographers* (Cham: Palgrave Macmillan, 2022), 113.

5 Jerold Frakes, "Vikings, Vínland and the Discourse of Eurocentrism", *Journal of English and Germanic Philology* 100, no. 2 (April 2001).

6 Pernille Hermann, "The Horror of Vínland: Topographies and Otherness in the Vínland sagas", *Scandinavian Studies* 93, no. 1 (April 2021). https://doi.org./10.5406/scanstud.93.1.0001.

7 Annette Lassen, "Vínland – Paradise or Pagan Periphery?", in *An Icelandic Florilegium: A Festschrift in Honor of Úlfar Bragason on his 70th Birthday*, eds. Kirsten Wolf and Marianne Kalinke (Ithaca: Cornell University Press, 2021).

8 Barnes, *Viking America*; Geraldine Barnes, "Nostalgia, medievalism and the Vínland voyages", *postmedieval: a journal of medieval cultural studies* vol. 2, no. 2 (June 2011). https://doi.org/10.1057/pmed.2011.2.

9 Helgason, *Echoes.*

10 Regal, *America's Origin*, 106, 109.

Rafn, he was an esteemed member of The Royal Nordic Society of Antiquaries (1825–).[11] Although the question of America's Norse origin grew in popularity later in the 19th century, Rafn's Viking theory would have resonated with some readers and theatre audiences in 1830s and 1840s Denmark, as more Scandinavians settled in America. In his play, Oehlenschläger directly addresses the concern for the preservation of Scandinavian heritage in the light of these first stages of emigration. As such, *Landet fundet og forsvundet* is a valuable contribution to the study of the Vinland voyages' post-medieval reception, which, given their impact on America's national identity, is primarily dominated by Anglophone studies.

The Vinland voyages' authenticity was not confirmed until the 1960s, when Norwegian archaeologists Helge and Anne Stine Ingstad excavated L'Anse aux Meadows in Newfoundland. The archaeological site revealed a settlement from around the year 1000, which contained remnants of eight Norse-style buildings used for both habitation and workshops. Due to the lack of burial sites, historians estimate that the settlement was not occupied for long.[12] In the 19th century, however, Norse settlements in North America was a disputed theory, and the location of Vinland varied between antiquarians. To account for this, this article will disregard the historical authenticity behind the Vinland voyages. Instead, they will be analyzed as examples of cultural memory. The same goes for *Landet fundet og forsvundet*, which in its essence is a metatextual and multilayered story about memory and preservation.

Based on philosopher Maurice Halbwach's *mémoire collective* (collective memory), Astrid Erll defines cultural memory as an 'interplay of present and past in socio-cultural context.'[13] As a concept, cultural memory relies on a constructed idea of a shared past. Within cultural memory studies, the past is not given, but rather continuously 're-constructed and re-presented.'[14] Jan Assman elaborates by separating cultural memory from communicative memory. While communicative memory is non-institutionalized and restricted to individuals and their interaction with contemporaries or next generations, cultural memory depends on institutions, whose agents vary over time and preserve and reembody memory.

11 *Antiquitates Americanæ* is included in *Bibliotheca Oehlenschlägeriana* (1850), though the book does not specify which year Oehlenschläger obtained the book. The aforementioned books by Peringskiöld, Torfæus, Mallet, Percy, and Forster are absent in his library, but he could have read or borrowed them.

12 Elanor Rosamund Barraclough, "The Great Viking Fake-Off: The Cultural Legacy of Norse Voyages to North America" in *The Vikings Reimagined*, eds. Tom Birkett & Roderick Dale (Berlin, Boston: Medieval Institute Publications, 2020), 254.

13 Astrid Erll, "Cultural Memory Studies: An Introduction", in *Cultural Memory Studies. An International and Interdisciplinary Handbook*, eds. Astrid Erll et.al. (Berlin: Walter de Gruyter, 2008), 2.

14 Erll, "Cultural Memory Studies", 7.

Institutions cast the past in symbols, such as oral myths, writings, and performances, thereby continually illuminating and changing the past in the present.[15]

Like some of his contemporaries, Oehlenschläger used the Vinland voyages to reconstruct and preserve a certain version of the medieval past. On the one hand, *Landet fundet og forsvundet* gives a nuanced glimpse into the 19th century's theories about Vinland. On the other hand, the play also exposes its author's own concerns for his legacy as a poet. To examine this combination of extroverted and introverted aspect of memory and preservation, the article focuses on the main character Biørn Asbrandson and particularly his monologue near the play's ending. The article's main argument is that Biørn displays Oehlenschläger's considerations regarding the memory of Vinland and the Old Norse legacy in the light of emerging emigration from Scandinavia to America. Through Biørn, Oehlenschläger addresses potential emigrants within his Danish audience and simultaneously portrays the poet as a crucial curator of memory. Like Biørn, the poet Oehlenschläger is an example of how agents preserve and reembody memory on behalf of institutions, such as national theatres or societies of antiquarians. As the article will demonstrate, this thematization of memory adds a metatextual layer to *Landet fundet og forsvundet.* In preparation for this analysis, the following section gives a more thorough introduction to the play as well as an overview of Oehlenschläger's main sources of inspiration. Surprisingly, the play does not rely on the narrative in the Vinland Sagas but is instead modelled after sections in *Eyrbyggja saga* (*Saga of the People of Eyri*).

Landet fundet og forsvundet: Story and inspiration

Oehlenschläger initiated his authorship with adaptations of medieval ballads and Old Norse literature. In Lund Cathedral 1829, he received the title as the poet king of the North. Later, in 1842, he became commander of the Order of Dannebrog (1671–), member of the Royal Netherlands Academy of Arts and Sciences (1808–) and was also awarded with a gold medal at the Swedish Academy (1786–) for his work with Old Norse history and mythology.[16] Oehlenschläger's fame and reputation as a poet and playwright was more than well-established, when he began writing *Landet fundet og forsvundet.* Not only does the play belong to his long list of works of medievalism; it also marks his renewed fascination with Old Norse literature after having written tragedies primarily inspired

15 Jan Assmann, "Communicative and Cultural Memory", in *Cultural Memory Studies. An International and Interdisciplinary Handbook*, eds. Astrid Erll et.al. (Berlin: Walter de Gruyter, 2008), 113.

16 Adam Oehlenschläger, *Oehlenschlägers Erindringer. Fierde Bind* (Copenhagen: Høst, 1851), 164–165.

by the high Middle Ages. Vilhelm Andersen explains that this part of Oehlenschläger's productivity was a response to Walter Scott and B.S. Ingemann whose works had popularized the medieval period since the 1820s.[17] Ida Falbe-Hansen has noticed that this poetic interest in the high Middle Ages changed for the older Oehlenschläger who instead came back to Old Norse literature. She links this reinvigoration to the year 1840 where Oehlenschläger stayed at Nysø with other artists and scholars, including N.F.S. Grundtvig, Bertel Thorvaldsen, and Henrik Steffens.[18] Paul Rubow adds that Oehlenschläger's relationship with the Royal Nordic Society of Antiquaries might have encouraged him to return to Old Norse material, which by the 1830–40s had been frequently updated with more modern translations.[19] Despite having adapted these stories and myths since his youth, Oehlenschläger was not fluent in the Old Norse language and therefore relied more on translations than some of his contemporaries.

With the prosaic collection *Nordiske Oldsagn* (Nordic Ancient Myths, 1840) and *Ørvarrods Saga* (The Saga of Ørvarrod, 1841), Oehlenschläger brought more mythic storytelling back into his authorship. *Landet fundet og forsvundet*, however, has more in common with his historical plays, as it contains no supernatural elements and takes place during the Christian conversion around the late 10th century. With dramas like *Hakon Jarl* (1807), *Palnatoke* (1809) and later *Olaf den Hellige* (Olav the Holy, 1838), Oehlenschläger was familiar with this period in Scandinavian history. Having read Snorre Sturluson's chronicle *Heimskringla* (c. 1230) already in his youth, Oehlenschläger might have been acquainted with the Vinland voyages many years before Rafn drew attention to the sagas with *Antiquitates Americanæ*.

Landet fundet og forsvundet differs from Oehlenschläger's other dramas in that it consists of a short prologue and only two acts instead of five. Each act takes place within one day separately but varies in terms of space and time: While the first is situated in Iceland, the second one unfolds in Vinland, 25 years later. During this time, we learn that Iceland has undergone Christian conversion like the rest of the North although this has not put a stop to violence and bloodshed. Regarding the play's timeframe, Oehlenschläger does not give a specific date. Judging by his sources, the acts are possibly set around the years 998 and 1023.

The prologue is a monologue by Ægir, entitled as the Norse god of the sea, who presents the Norsemen as forgotten explorers that predated Columbus by 500 years. First act introduces the main character, the skald and adventurer

---

17 Vilhelm Andersen, *Det nittende Aarhundredes første Halvdel* (Copenhagen: Gyldendal, 1924), 72ff.

18 Ida Falbe-Hansen, *Øhlenschlægers nordiske Digtning og andre Afhandlinger* (Copenhagen: Aschehoug & Co., 1921), 28.

19 Paul Rubow, *Saga og Pastiche. Bidrag til dansk prosahistorie* (Copenhagen: Gyldendal, 1968/1923), 75.

Biørn Asbrandson, who has just returned to Iceland and tells of exploits. He has met famous kings and travelled to the South, though he concludes that none of his journeys can compete with his home. He has longed for Thuride, daughter of Snorre, and his foster sister whom he greets with a gift: the last one of two golden arm rings. He tells her that he threw the first one to an unknown Norseman who saved him on the sea. Due to the thick fog, Biørn could not see his face on the deck. While handing her the arm ring, Biørn declares his love, only to learn that she is engaged to Thorkild Eigilson, a man chosen by her father and who may return to Iceland at any moment. When Thorkild arrives soon after, Biørn decides to challenge him to a duel. Before the fight begins, Thorkild gives Thuride a golden arm ring identical to Biørn's as a wedding gift, and she immediately shares this surprise with Biørn. Discovering that Thorkild was the stranger who saved his life, Biørn withdraws from the duel and gives Thuride and Thorkild his blessings, and leaves Iceland in search for Vinland.

Second act opens with a group of Norsemen arriving in Vinland. They are led by Biørn the Young whose company includes Halfdan the Old, Sigmund, and the two slaves Leif and Didrik, a German. A group of Skraelings perform a warrior dance and threaten the Norsemen with arrows and maces. However, the conflict is stopped by what appears to be the Skraelings' chieftain; an old man with white hair called Quetfalcoalt[20]. He carries a sword and a golden chain and turns out to be an old Icelander who came to Vinland 25 years ago and lost his companions. Although the Skraelings believe him to be a god, he calls them deceitful and tells Biørn the Young and his men to leave immediately. Biørn the Young reveals in his dialogue with Quetfalcoalt that he is the son of Thorkild and Thuride who unfortunately died one year after his birth. Thorkild has since remarried, and Iceland has converted to Christianity. Quetfalcoalt gives Biørn the Young his sword and chain, asking him to return to Vinland with more men and spread the Nordic language. After their exchange, Halfdan the Old tells Biørn that the old man is Biørn Asbrandson who treasured Thuride. Just before he leaves Vinland's shores, Biørn the Young places Thuride's golden arm ring on a big rock. The play ends with Biørn Asbrandson who, led by two Skraeling boys, reads the ring's inscription out loud: 'Min kiære, stadige Tanke!'[21] (My dear, constant Thought).

As the summary suggests, neither *Eiríks saga rauða* nor *Grænlendinga saga* are the main inspiration behind the play's narrative.[22] Rather, the play follows

20 The name is likely based on Quetzalcoatl, an important Aztec deity and patron god of Aztec priesthood.

21 Adam Oehlenschläger, *Landet fundet og forsvundet* (Copenhagen: Høst, 1846), 58.

22 Falbe-Hansen suggest that *Laxdæla saga* is another source of inspiration (Falbe-Hansen, *Øhlenschlægers*, 67). Others might include *Bjarnar saga Hítdælakappa* (*The Saga of Björn, Champion of the Hitardal People*) and *Gunnlaugs saga ormstunga* (*Saga of Gunnlaugur Serpent-Tongue*). Both sagas feature exchanges of golden rings and centre around two men

specific parts of *Eyrbyggja saga*, a saga of Icelanders that has survived in multiple manuscripts from the 14th century. In the year 1845, the saga had been available in Latin and Danish for decades.[23] Oehlenschläger owned different versions of the saga in the form of Peter Erasmus Müller's *Sagabibliothek* (Saga Library, 1817), Finnur Magnússon and Rafn's *Grönlands historiske Mindesmærker* (Greenland's historical Memorials, 1838), Rafn's *Antiquitates Americanæ*, and Henry Wheaton's *History of the Northmen* (1831).[24] While Müller's and Wheaton's books are more retellings than literal translations, they share an important feature with Magnússon and Rafn: All four interpret *Eyrbyggja saga* as a testimony to the existence of Vinland even though the place name is never mentioned in the saga.

The specific section in question from *Eyrbyggja saga* is the story about Bjorn Asbrandsson, also known as Bjorn *Breiðvikinga-kappi*.[25] In *Grönlands historiske Mindesmærker*, his story within the saga is highlighted with its own subtitle. Magnússon and Rafn explain that they have supplemented earlier manuscripts, including those used by Müller, with overlooked catalogues from the Arnamagnæan manuscript collection that contain further information about the character.[26] While the saga briefly mentions Thorfinn Karlsefni's journey to Vinland and his feuds with the Skraelings, Bjorn's journey is more mysterious. He visits Thuride so often that he is assaulted by her husband Thorodd. After killing some of Thorodd's men, Bjorn is banished for three years. Upon his return, he remarks that Thuride's son Kjartan looks more like him than Thorodd. He is then ordered to stop seducing Thuride and he leaves Iceland never to return. Later, the Norseman Gudleif Gudlaugson is driven west and reaches an unknown land where the natives seize him and his men. The natives' white-haired chieftain,

competing for a woman who marries one while the other is at sea. For the sake of the focus in this article, I have chosen to prioritize Oehlenschläger's adaptation of *Eyrbyggja saga* and parts of the Vinland Sagas.

23 A Latin translation of the saga was written by G. J. Thorkelin and published by the Arnamagmæan Commission in 1787, based on a transcript by Árni Magnússon and sponsored by P.F. Suhm.

24 Louis Klein (publisher), *Bibliotheca Oehlenschlägeriana* (Copenhagen: Louis Klein, 1850), 46, 49, 6, 47. Another Danish translation of *Eyrbyggja saga* by N. M. Petersen was published in 1844 as part of his series of Icelandic sagas. Since Oehlenschläger was in Paris in 1844–1845, I estimate that he did not read this version and have therefore omitted it from my analysis. Oehlenschläger would possibly also have been familiar with Scott's rendition of the saga from *Illustrations of Nordic Antiquities* (1814), which Müller also notices in his postscript to *Eyrbyggja* saga. According to *Bibliotheca Oehlenschlägeriana* (1850) though, Oehlenschläger did not own Scott's version from 1814.

25 In order to distinguish between the saga character and Oehlenschläger's version, the article uses the name Bjorn Asbrandsson to refer to the character from the saga, while Biørn Asbrandson refers to the character in Oehlenschläger's play.

26 Finnur Magnússon and C.C. Rafn, *Grönlands historiske Mindesmærker. Förste Bind* (Copenhagen: Det Brünnichske Trykkeri, 1838), 505–509.

however, who speaks Norse, asks Gudleif about Thuride and Kjartan and hands over gifts to Gudleif, but he won't reveal his name. Only when Gudleif arrives in Iceland, people speculate about whether the old man was the infamous warrior and skald Bjorn Asbrandsson.

Oehlenschläger follows this plot loosely and has reduced the number of characters, altered some of their names and changed their relationships to one another. He has particularly favoured the love triangle yet made his version of Bjorn less confrontational and more tender. His love for Thuride is 'purer' as he does not seduce her while she is married but ends up accepting her betrothal to Thorkild. According to Falbe-Hansen, this battle between Nordic ethics and alluring love is a central theme in the play. She also writes that Oehlenschläger changed the saga material to such an extent that 'man maa snarere sige, at det er noget, der kunne være sket, end at det *er* det' (one ought preferably to say that it is something that could have happened, rather than something that *did* happen).[27]

Unlike many other post-medieval adaptations of the Vinland voyages, Oehlenschläger deliberately prioritizes *Eyrbyggja saga* over the Vinland Sagas, whose narratives are secondary in his play. But his interpretation of Bjorn's final days in Vinland is in fact consistent with theories from contemporary translators and editors: Müller ends *Eyrbyggja saga* with the following statement: 'Denne Fortælling bærer Sanddruhedens Præg. Landet, hvortil Gudleif blev fordrevet, kan ikke være andet end Amerika. Eller én af de vestindiske Øer' (This Tale is characterized by Truth. The Land, from which Gudleif was driven away, cannot be anywhere else than America. Or one of the West Indies).[28] Wheaton implies the same interpretation as he sums up Bjorn's journey in connection with a presentation of the Vinland Sagas in chapter two of *History of the Northmen.* In a footnote, Wheaton even proposes that Vinland is at the 'latitude of Boston, the present capital of New England'.[29] Wheaton might have favoured this location for personal reasons as he was born in Providence, Rhode Island, in New England. In their introduction to *Eyrbyggja saga*, Magnússon and Rafn write that Bjorn 'tilbragne sine senere Leveaar i Amerika som de Indfödtes Hövding' (spent his latter Years in America as the Natives' Chieftain).[30] In the list of characters' genealogy, Magnússon and Rafn estimate that Björn lived in America from 999 to

27 Falbe-Hansen, *Øhlenschlægers*, 67.

28 Peter Erasmus Müller, *Sagabibliothek, med Anmærkninger og indledende Afhandlinger. Første Bind* (Copenhagen: J. F. Schulz, 1817), 194.

29 Henry Wheaton, *History of the Northmen, or Danes and Normans, from the Earliest Times to the Conquest of England by William of Normandy* (London: John Murray, Albemarle Street, 1831), 24.

30 Magnússon and Rafn, *Grönlands*, 509.

1027.[31] Rafn does not supply his translation of Bjorn Asbrandsson's story with such a statement in *Antiquitates Americanæ*. Like Wheaton, however, he strongly implies that the land Bjorn and Gudleif encounter is indeed Vinland since he includes specific parts of *Eyrbyggja saga* in the section 'Breviores relationes' along with other medieval sources related to Vinland. This a good example of how Rafn presents his arguments both directly in written text and indirectly via *Antiquitates Americanæ*'s paratext.[32] A more metatextual method is used by Oehlenschläger who, in *Landet fundet og forsvundet* incorporates Rafn's Viking theory in a variety of ways, thereby giving the memory of Vinland a sense of authenticity.

Creating a misplaced Biørn and an 'authentic' Vinland

References to the Vinland voyages appear differently in each act: The first one establishes the knowledge of Leif Erikson's and Thorfinn Karlsefni's settlements via dialogue while the second act takes place in Vinland itself. Oehlenschläger uses a variation of the narrative technique 'show, don't tell' by presenting Vinland in the form of 'tell first, then show'. By depicting Vinland through the eyes of both a young and an old Biørn Asbrandson, Oehlenschläger unifies the acts despite their differences in place and time. Oehlenschläger also makes sure to tie the theme of memory to his main character, thereby making him likable and relatable for a modern audience.

In act one, Biørn summarizes parts of the Vinland Sagas during a conversation with his friend Steen: 'Før hiem vi drog, du foreslog mig, først at gaae / Paa Eventyr, Opdagerreiser. Skiønne Land, / Af Leif og Thorfin fundet alt – hvor Vinen groer –'[33] (Before vi went home, you suggested that I should go first / On Adventure, Voyages. To the beautiful Land, / Found by Leif and Thorfin – where the Wine grows –). By including these passages, Oehlenschläger establishes the fact that Vinland is well known and that some from the expedition has already been killed or returned.[34] He also uses the references to reveal the adventurous

31 Magnússon and Rafn, *Grönlands*, 789.

32 I borrow this term from Gérard Genette, who uses it to define a book's physicality. According to Genette, the paratext is what connects a text to its socio-historical surroundings, i. e., the readers and publishers. The paratext reveals how a text depends on literary systems and cultures (Gérard Genette, *Paratexts. Thresholds of interpretation* (Cambridge: Cambridge University Press, 1997/1987), 407, 1ff).

33 Oehlenschläger, *Landet*, 14.

34 If Oehlenschläger was aware of Magnússon and Rafn's theory about the date of Bjorn Asbrandsson's stay in America (999–1027), he must also have known that this time frame collides with *Antiquitates Americanæ*, where Rafn dates Leif's arrival in Vinland to the year

and curious elements in Biørn's character and that the memory of the Vinland voyages fascinates him deeply. Later, the audience also discovers his cunningness and playful use of words as he expresses his interest in Vinland in a sarcastic comment to Thorkild who has visited the place. Thorkild mentions that he took reindeer skins from the Skraelings and later met a foe on the sea to which Biørn remarks: 'Beskedne Thorkild, nævn hans Navn!'[35] (Modest Thorkild, say his Name!). The foe in question was a whale that Thorkild managed to kill with a harpoon 'lykkeligt og dybt'[36] (happily and deeply). This encounter is partially based on the Vinland sagas' Thorfinn Karlsefni who finds a beached whale with his fellow explorers and gives milk in exchange for the Skraelings' precious skins.[37] Oehlenschläger has turned this trade into a raid and the beached whale into a whaling episode to underline the juxtaposition of greed and bravery in Thorkild's character.[38] His exchange with Biørn also foreshadows the revelation that he is Biørn's mysterious rescuer; a friend, not 'En Fiende jeg paa Havet traf, som var mig værd'[39] (A worthy Foe I met on the Sea).

Oehlenschläger particularly elaborates on Biørn's character by contrasting him with Thorkild in the first act: Despite proving to have a strong sense of honour, Thorkild sometimes appears as a caricature of the self-made man. He proudly tells Thuride of his wealth and openly admits that he only asked for her hand because of her fortune. His salute to Biørn before the duel is even reminiscent of a liberal laissez-faire logic: 'Hver haaber Lykken' (Every Man hopes for Fortune).[40] Thorkild considers Biørn childish because of his strong feelings and is confused whenever Biørn uses 'Skialdesprog'[41] (Skaldic language) to express himself. In return, Biørn is more impulsive and responsive to the power of memory: When he first enters the stage, Biørn announces his happiness to see the Icelandic hall again, though it is 'Lidt mindre vistnok nu end før, da jeg som Dreng / Halvvoxen sad; da dobbelt stor du tykkes mig.'[42] (A bit smaller perhaps now than before, when I as a Boy / Adolescent sat here; then you seemed to be twice as big). Biørn then continues to reminisce about 'Fædrenes Bedrifter'[43]

1000 (C. C. Rafn, *Antiquitates Americanæ* (Copenhagen: Schultz, 1837), xxix). This would explain why Oehlenschläger chose not to include a specific date in the play.

35 Oehlenschläger, *Landet*, 22.
36 Oehlenschläger, *Landet*, 22.
37 Rafn, *Antiquitates*, 57ff.
38 Thorkild's whaling can also be read as a reference to the whaling industry, which peaked in 1840s America and was later immortalized in Herman Melville's *Moby-Dick* (1851).
39 Oehlenschläger, *Landet*, 22.
40 Oehlenschläger, *Landet*, 24.
41 Oehlenschläger, *Landet*, 23.
42 Oehlenschläger, *Landet*, 9.
43 Oehlenschläger, *Landet*, 9.

(The Deeds of the Fathers) as well as the myths about Odin and Thor, that he heard in a reading of *Völuspá.*

Already in this introduction, Oehlenschläger stresses that Biørn is driven by his memories, some of which tend to paint the past in a more idyllic image. After giving his last arm ring to Thuride, Biørn recounts his journey in a monologue in which he continually repeats how, when abroad, he often thought: 'Det var alt Andet hiemme, da paa Island du / I Hallen hos Thuride sad; og bedre bli'er / Det først, naar du hos hende sidder der igien.'[44] (It was nothing but Home, when you on Iceland / In the Hall sat with Thuride; and better it will be / Only, when you sit there with her again.). With lines like these, Oehlenschläger tells his audience that memory is a driving force behind Biørn's actions. His memory of Thuride drove him back to Iceland and his memory of the Vinland voyages later drives him back to the seas. Whereas Thorkild seems to expose aspects of modernity and its capitalistic logic, in a post-medieval and anachronistic fashion, Biørn is instead caught between the past and the present: Since boyhood, he has been captivated by ancient stories and despite his accomplishments abroad, the memory of Thuride made him homesick. He regrets that he did not take her hand 'til rette Tid'[45] (in due Time), and laments that his poetic visions cannot be reconciled with 'Virkelighedens ynkelige, magre Land'[46] (Reality's pathetic, barren Land). In other words, Biørn is aware of the differences between reality and his imagination and this knowledge leaves him feeling misplaced wherever he goes. He is especially out of touch as an old man in the second act: While the rest of Scandinavia has embraced Christianity, which Biørn also sympathizes with, he remains a heathen and declines Biørn the Young's offer to baptize him. Much like Thorkild, Biørn the Young also has trouble understanding the old Biørn: 'Jeg ei forstaaer din Tale, Gubbe, veed ei ret, / Hvortil den sigter.'[47] (I do not understand your Speech, Greybeard, I do not know, / Whereto it aims). By displaying Biørn's nostalgic traits already in the first act, Oehlenschläger makes him vulnerable and perhaps more relatable to a 19th century audience who would recognize Biørn's fondness of Norse mythology as well as his excitement about Vinland/America.

Act two turns Biørn into a living and breathing memory in his own right, thereby underpinning the play's metatextual element. The second act also relies more distinctly on Rafn's scholarship, as it refers to artefacts and buildings in America that, according to Rafn and others, proved that Norsemen discovered America. These references are: The Newport Tower on Rhode Island, a skeleton found at Fall River, Massachusetts, and the Assonet stone, also known as the Dighton

44 Oehlenschläger, *Landet*, 12.
45 Oehlenschläger, *Landet*, 19.
46 Oehlenschläger, *Landet*, 17.
47 Oehlenschläger, *Landet*, 46.

Rock, located at the Taunton River, Massachusetts. All three merge in the final scene of *Landet fundet og forsvundet* where the old Biørn announces to the Skraeling boys, that they must bury him underneath a rock wearing Thuride's ring. Out of the three artefacts, only Dighton Rock has been noticed by Falbe-Hansen who suggests that the rock, which Oehlenschläger would have encountered in *Antiquitates Americanæ*'s sketches and letters, served as inspiration for Biørn's burial place in the final scene.[48] However, Oehlenschläger also includes the Newport Tower and the skeleton albeit in a more indirect fashion.

Neither Newport Tower nor the Fall River skeleton are to be found in *Antiquitates Americanæ* though Rafn was aware of both when Oehlenschläger wrote *Landet fundet og forsvundet:* Rafn wrote intensively about Newport Tower in Rhode Island in his 1841-supplement to *Antiquitates Americanæ* as well as in an article published in *Annaler for nordisk Oldkyndighed* (Annals for Nordic Antiquity) the same year. This building was first mentioned in the will of Benedict Arnold from 1678 and referred to as an 'Old Stone Mill'[49]. Though later scholars have confirmed that the tower indeed stems from a 17th century mill, Rafn posited that the building was built on a foundation dating back to pre-Columbian times. Based on drawings sent to him by the artist Frederick Catherwood and accounts from Thomas Webb, secretary of the Rhode Island Historical Society (1822–), Rafn states that this building was erected no later than the 12th century and is of Nordic origin.[50] As a counter argument to Webb who suggested that the building was originally a watch tower, Rafn argues that it must have had 'a hellig Bestemmelse' (a holy Purpose).[51] To validate this claim, he compares Newport Tower to churches and crypts in Vestervig, Viborg, Sorø, and Bornholm, hoping that future studies will prove whether masses were sung in Old Norse seven hundred years ago.[52]

A couple of lines in *Landet fundet og forsvundet* possibly confirm that Oehlenschläger was familiar with Rafn's theory about Newport Tower's Norse origin: When the old Biørn reveals his Norse identity to Biørn the Young and his men, he explains that the Skraelings see him as a god. After they killed the rest of his expedition, including Steen, he taught the Skraelings how to build 'bedre Hytter' (better Huts)[53] and to harvest the earth with 'Ploug og Harv'[54] (Plow and Harrow).

48 Falbe-Hansen, *Øhlenschlægers*, 67.

49 C. C. Rafn, *Supplement to the Antiquitates Americanæ* (Copenhagen: The Royal Society of Northern Antiquaries, 1841, 3.

50 Rafn, *Supplement*, 15.

51 C. C. Rafn, "Bemærkninger om en gammel Bygning i Newport paa Rhode-Island, Nordboernes Viinland", *Annaler for nordisk Oldkyndighed,* 3, (Copenhagen: J. D. Qvist, 1841), 46.

52 Rafn, "Bemærkninger", 51.

53 Oehlenschläger, *Landet*, 44.

54 Oehlenschläger, *Landet*, 44.

Biørn, however, refuses to live with them and wear their clothes. Instead, he explains: 'Paa Høien hist i Eensomhed min Hytte staaer; / Did ile stundom de, som til et Gudehuus, / At hente Raad.'[55] (On the Hill yonder in Loneliness stands my Hut / They sometimes hurry, as if it were a God House, / To gather Advice). Biørn, acting as a form of master builder, suggests that his hut is built after Norse traditions and could be a reference to Newport Tower. Contrary to Rafn, who presumed that the tower was built to worship the Christian god, Oehlenschläger perhaps includes the tower to underline the Skraelings' superstition: It is a 'Gudehuus' ('God House') only in their eyes, and since Biørn Asbrandson is a pagan, it becomes a more exotic building, made by heathen Norse and Skraeling hands.

Biørn's declaration of his burial underneath the rock can be another reference to an American artefact, the skeleton at Fall River: Unearthed in 1832 but destroyed in a fire in 1843, the skeleton was found in a sitting position with a brass plate covering its breast.[56] Some of the remains were even sent to Denmark for inspection with the assumption that it came from a Norse burial.[57] Henry Wadsworth Longfellow immortalized this mysterious finding in his famous poem "The Skeleton in Armor" (1841) which includes a more direct reference to Newport Tower. Longfellow had visited the tower himself and quotes Rafn's theory about its Norse origin in his introduction to the poem in *Ballads and Other Poems* (1842). The poem itself also includes the building as the narrator, a long-forgotten Viking, tells how he built a 'lofty tower'[58] to himself and his lover and buried her underneath it. As Carolyne Larrington notes in her recent book, *The Norse Myths that Shape the Way we Think* from 2022, Longfellow's poem bluntly claims that the 'first American of European heritage is of Norse stock.'[59]

Though Longfellow's works are nowhere to be found in Oehlenschläger's library, he might have heard about the "Skeleton in armor" or the poem of the same name via the Royal Nordic Society of Antiquaries: During his European tour, Longfellow visited Copenhagen in 1835 and met Rafn who gave him lessons in Icelandic and nominated him for membership in the society.[60] With its admiration for the Norse courage and defiance of death, Longfellow's poem is reminiscent of 'Gothic' or 'Runic' poems from Thomas Gray and Thomas Percy. Like Longfellow, Oehlenschläger provides a romantic context for the skeleton

55 Oehlenschläger, *Landet*, 44.

56 Regal, *America's Origin*, 126–127.

57 William E. Fitzhugh and Elisabeth I. Ward, "Celebrating the Viking Past: A Viking Millennium in America" in *Vikings: The North Atlantic Saga*, eds. William E. Fitzhugh and Elisabeth I. Ward (Washington and London: Smithsonian Institution Press, 2000), 352.

58 Henry Wadsworth Longfellow, *Ballads and other Poems* (Cambridge: John Owen, 1842), 39.

59 Carolyne Larrington, *The Norse Myths that shape the Way we Think* (London: Thames & Hudson Ltd, 2022), 236.

60 Andrew Hilen (ed.), *The Letters of Henry Wadsworth Longfellow. Volume 1: 1814–1836* (Cambridge: Harvard University Press, 2013), 515.

and presents it as evidence of a Norse burial in medieval America. In the play, this burial has not yet taken place but is hinted at in Biørn's final and prophetic words. Regardless of whether Oehlenschläger or Longfellow believed in Rafn's theories about the Vinland voyages or not, works like *Antiquitates Americanæ* stimulated their imagination. Both authors used supposedly 'Norse' remains in America to make their works historically believable and topical at the same time.

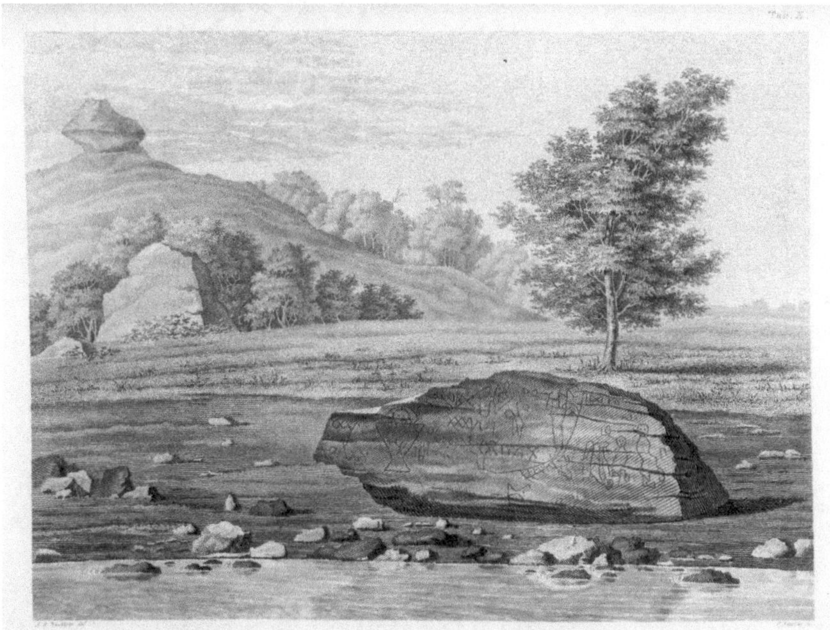

VIEW OF THE ASSONET INSCRIPTION ROCK.

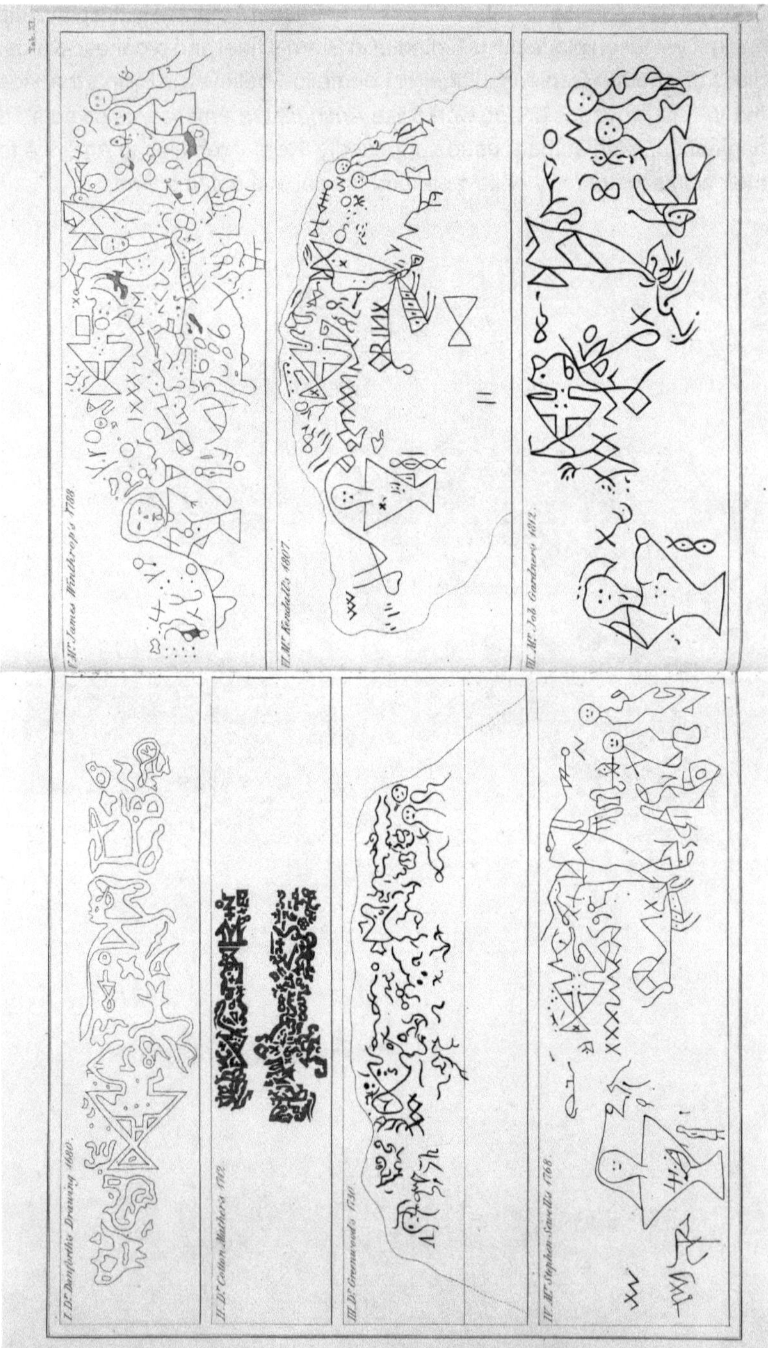
I. Dr. Danforths Drawing 1680.
II. Dr. Cotton Mathers 1712.
III. Dr. Greenwoods 1730.
IV. Mr. Stephen Sewells 1768.
V. Mr. James Winthrop's 1788.
VI. Mr. Kendall's 1807.
VII. Mr. Job Gardners 1812.

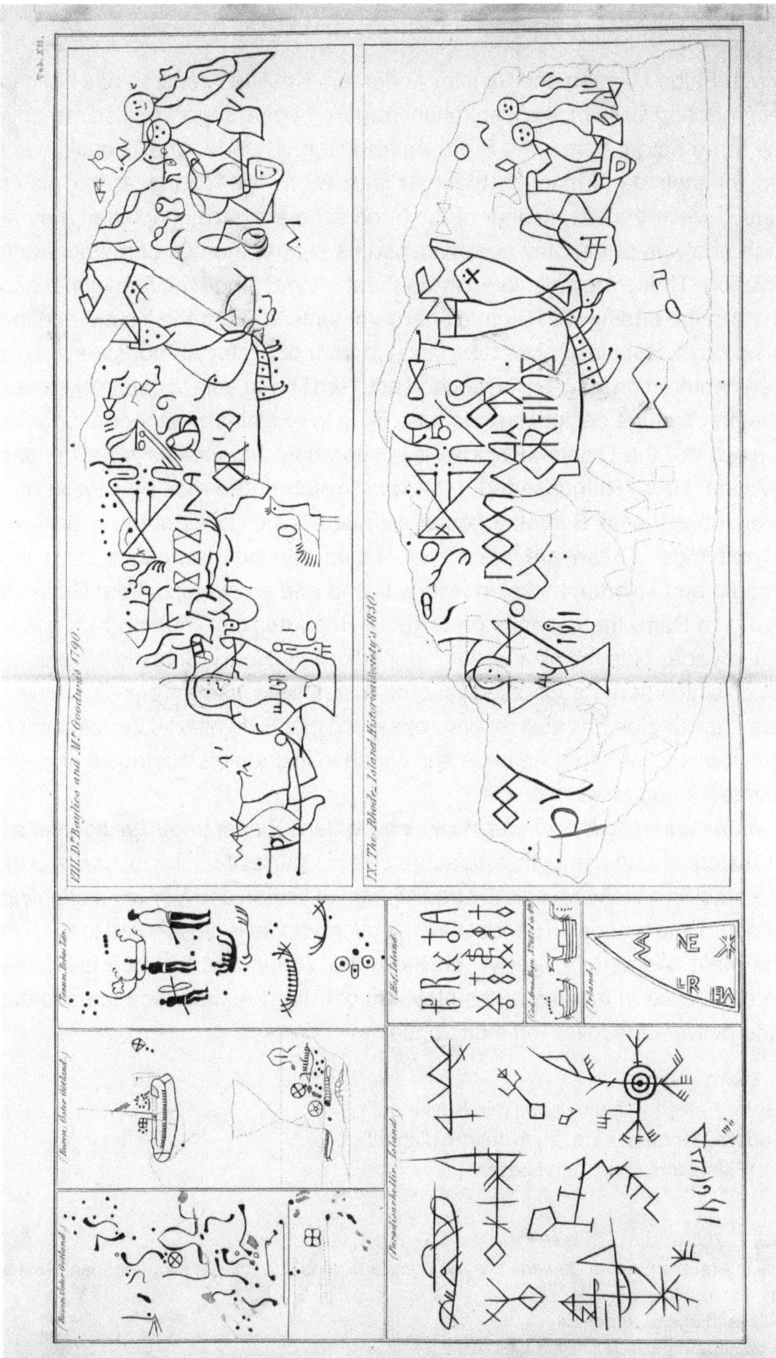
VIII. Dr. Baylies and Mr. Goodwin's 1790.
IX. The Rhode Island Historical Society's 1830.

The value of memory

Along with Falbe-Hansen and Vilhelm Andersen, Kristian Arentzen has noticed *Landet fundet og forsvundets* inspiration from *Eyrbyggja saga.* He also remarks that the three actors portraying Biørn Asbrandson, Thuride, and Thorkild were praised for their performances together with Biørn the Young at the play's premiere.[61] Nevertheless, neither of the three scholars have conducted a more thorough analysis of the play nor examined its central themes of memory and preservation. These are articulated throughout *Landet fundet og forsvundet* and culminate in the ending with Biørn's final comments to Biørn the Young and the Skraeling boys. Both instances take place in front of a 'stor Kampesteen'[62] (big Boulder) centered on stage in the second act. Had I been able to obtain sketches from the play's stage design, I would have liked to examine whether the boulder was formed like the Dighton Rock as it appeared in *Antiquitates Americanæ*'s final section. Here, Rafn inserted a detailed sketch of the rock by linguist and historian John Russell Bartlett together with detailed pictures of the rock's unknown carvings. These are placed alongside similar inscriptions from the Portsmouth and Tiverton rocks on Rhode Island and an example from Gotland. According to Rafn, the carvings on Dighton Rock depicts Thorfinn Karlsefni's Vinland voyage. This theory was later debunked by Henry Schoolcraft among others, of which some suggested that the inscriptions came from Algonquian peoples.[63] Larrington has also recently observed that Rafn altered the inscription sketches he received from America and chose to include his altered versions in *Antiquitates Americanæ.*[64]

In *Landet fundet og forsvundet,* however, Oehlenschäger treats the boulder as both a historical and symbolic artefact to suit his narrative. Like in *Hakon Jarl*, where a crack in a stone reveals the fragile reign of Hakon and Norway's crippling heathendom, the boulder in *Landet fundet og forsvundet* is closely tied to the plot and the main character's fate. When Biørn the Young and his men leave the shores of Vinland at the end of the play, the old Biørn Asbrandson turns to the rock and delivers the following monologue:

Biørn
Farvel, Farvel! – O kom igien, min Navne du!
Og udbred Nordens Ære, styrk dets Herlighed!
[Skibet forsvinder bag Næsset.]

61 Kristian Arentzen, *Adam Oehlenschläger. Literaturhistorisk Livsbillede* (Copenhagen: Høst & Søn, 1879), 489.
62 Oehlenschläger, *Landet*, 34.
63 Linderoth and Fitzhugh, "Stumbles", 378.
64 Larrington, *Myths*, 233.

Biørn

[mørk, stirrende hen for sig.]

Men – sorte Skyer true fælt Synsfredsen mig!
Jeg seer i Aanden Loke sig forsvandt med Ran,
At spærre Veien for det modige Kæmpeværk.
Ja, Utgaards fæle Drømmetrold: Uvidenhed!
I Taagedamp, med tætte Slør for Øinene,
Inddysser raske Forsæt du. – Erindringen
Om dette Tog forsvinder uden Virkning. – Snart
Veed Ingen meer, at her er Land, som venter ham. –
O, men paa denne store Steen, som staaer ved Strand,
Som Bølgen stundom overskyller i Flodens Tid,

Men Solen brænder tør igien, naar Ebben kom,
Jeg Runer hugge vil om vor Opdagelse,
Som Sol forvittre, Bølgen ei bortvaske skal.

[Til en af Drengene:]

Hent Huggejern og Hammer mig![65]

(**Biørn**

Goodbye, Goodbye! – O come back, you, my Name!
And spread the Honour of the North, strengthen its Glory!

[The Ship disappears behind the Headland.]

Biørn

[dark, starring in front of him.]

But – dark Clouds vilely threaten my Vision!
I see how Loki in spirit disappeared with Ran,
Blocking the Way for the courageous Giant Deed
Yes, the foul Dream Troll from Utgard: Ignorance!
In foggy Haze with thick Veil covering the Eyes,
You, lively Intention, lulled to Sleep. – The Memory
Of this Raid vanishes without any Effect. – Soon
No one will know here is Land that awaits him. –
O, but on this big Rock, which stands at the Shore,
Which the Waves sometimes drenches in the Time of the Flood,
But is burned dry with the Sun, once the Ebb Tide comes,
I will carve Runes about our Discovery,
As the Sun withers, the Waves shall never wash it away.

[To one of the Boys:]

Fetch me an iron Chisel and Hammer!)

With its poetic language and references to Norse mythology, the monologue underlines Biørn's heathendom and poetic sensibilities as a skald. Most importantly, these lines incapsulate the play's central theme of memory. Like the

65 Oehlenschläger, *Landet*, 55–56.

rock on stage, the 'Erindring' ('Memory') in Biørn's lines can be interpreted in different ways.

The first and most obvious form of memory in question is the memory of the Norse discovery of Vinland itself, the 'Togt' ('Raid'). Biørn's monologue mirrors Ægir's prologue, as he foresees and laments that the memory of the Norsemen's accomplishment 'forsvinder uden Virkning.' ('Vanishes without any effect'). In true skaldic fashion, he uses mythological characters, the deceitful Loki, and Ran, Ægir's wife, to explain that 'Uvidenhed' ('Ignorance') will follow his fellow Norsemen on their journey back home. Like 'Taagedamp med tætte Slør for Øinene', ('foggy Haze with thick Veil covering the Eyes') everyone will forget about Vinland and the Norsemen's brave discovery. Biørn, therefore, concludes that it is up to him to preserve the ill-fated memory the only way he can: By carving runes 'paa denne store Steen, som staaer ved Strand' ('on this big Rock, which stands at the Shore').

This is a throwback to the end of act one where Biørn writes a farewell to Thuride on a shield before leaving Iceland. Oehlenschläger once again lets Biørn put his knowledge of runes into practice in act two, thereby turning the boulder on stage into an actual archaeological object in today's America, the Dighton Rock.

The 'store Steen' ('big Rock') can also be read as a metatextual comment about the play itself: As Biørn declares, the stone will certainly be marked by time and the elements, but neither the sun nor the waves will 'bortvaske' ('wash away') the runes; the memory that is. The same can be said about *Landet fundet og forsvundet:* By narrating the story about Vinland, the play has brought a long-forgotten memory back to life. Biørn's work with 'Huggejern og Hammer' ('Iron Chisel and Hammer') might also refer to Oehlenschläger himself who, like his main character, takes on the role of a curator of memory. Instead of carving the memory of Vinland into a rock, Oehlenschläger turns it into a heroic play about the Norsemen's 'modige Kæmpeværk' ('courageous Giant Deed').

Soon after, in what is most likely a reference to the skeleton in armour, Biørn posits that his remains will put an end to future generation's ignorance about the discovery of Vinland: 'engang, om flere hundred Aar maaskee, / Paa denne Strand mand finde gamle Runesteen, / Og undre sig, og grave rundt, opdage meer. / Saa skue de min Beenrad med den gyldne Ring'[66] ('once, in perhaps several Hundred Years, / On this Beach they will find the old Rune Stone, / And wonder, and, upon digging, discover more. / Then they behold my Bones with the golden ring'). Oehlenschläger lets Biørn express himself in a prophetic fashion as he correctly predicts that people in 'flere hundred Aar' ('several Hundred Years') will discover his skeleton nearby the Dighton Rock. Audiences familiar with Rafn's theories and the skeleton uncovered in 1832 would easily understand

66 Oehlenschläger, *Landet*, 57–58.

Oehlenschläger's implication. Like the rune stone, Biørn's own body unlocks a memory that history has unfortunately forgotten: 'Saa vide de, at Nordens Mænd fandt dette Land, / Før Andre kom; og muligt saadan vriste vi / Den Ære, som tilkommer os, af fremmed Haand.'[67] ('Then they will know, that Men of the North found this Land, / Before others came; and perhaps then we will prize / The Honour we deserve, from Foreign Hand'). The play ends shortly after these lines, in which Biørn repeats Ægir's monologue by presenting the Norsemen as the true discoverers of America. *Landet fundet og forsvundet* almost quotes Rafn's *Antiquitates Americanæ* as it begins and ends with the hope that 'Nordens Mænd' ('The Men of the North') will finally be given the honour they deserve but which has hitherto been bestowed upon Columbus by foreign historians, 'Fremmed Haand' ('Foreign Hands').

Biørn's final monologues are examples of how Oehlenschläger thematizes memory within the play's props and dialogue and uses both to form a metatextual comment about the play itself. Particularly Biørn seems to be a mouthpiece for Oehlenschläger who uses this main character to address a contemporary audience. Vilhelm Andersen has also suggested that the old Biørn is an expression of an aging Oehlenschläger.[68] Given Oehlenschläger's status in 1840s' Scandinavia as a poet king of the North, he could easily identify with the old skald Biørn Asbrandson who reflects on his own poetic legacy and the poet's valuable relationship with memory. Andersen also appears to be the only scholar who draws attention to the contemporary emigration to America as an interesting context albeit he does not pursue this angle in his short analysis. However, when taking into consideration the rise of European emigration in the first half of the 19th century, the theme of memory in old Biørn's lines becomes even more topical and further reveals the play's metatextual meaning. When he bids the young Biørn goodbye, he exclaims his hope that Scandinavian men will soon appear on the shore of Vinland:

Snart venter jeg af norske, danske, svenske Mænd,
En vældig Flok, naar næstegang vi atter sees.
Her har I Plads nok; her indskrænkes ei af Iis (...)
Her I kan skabe Norden stort, (...)
sprede Sproget ud.
Farvel, Farvel! – O glemmer ei Quetfalcoalt![69]

(Soon I expect Norwegian, Danish, Swedish Men,
A mighty Group, the next Time we meet.

67 Oehlenschläger, *Landet*, 58.

68 Vilhelm Andersen, *Adam Oehlenschläger. Et Livs Poesi. Manddom og Alderdom* (Copenhagen: Det nordiske Forlag, 1899), 376.

69 Oehlenschläger, *Landet*, 54.

> Here you have Room enough; here you will not be entrapped by Ice (…)
> Here you can create the North greatly, (…)
> spread the Language.
> Goodbye, Goodbye! – O don't forget Quetfalcoalt!)

Biørn's hope shatters in his final monologue where he decides to preserve the memory on the rune stone himself. While Biørn in the play will never meet another Norseman, his lines above can be read as a direct call to 19th century Scandinavians who set sail for America. As Arentzen writes, *Landet fundet og forsvundet* is a celebration of Scandinavism.[70] In the midst of rising emigration, the concern for Scandinavian identity and its preservation must likely have been on Oehlenschläger's mind, and he uses his main character to display this: The old Biørn expects that future Scandinavians will 'sprede Sproget ud', ('spread the language') and 'skabe Norden stort' ('create the North greatly') in America. Him asking Biørn the Young and his men to not forget his name can even be interpreted as a reminder to 19th century Scandinavian emigrants who must remember their roots and plant a Nordic seed in America. Oehlenschläger might have chosen to adapt the story of Vinland to assure his countrymen that America was not a foreign country but in fact a long-forgotten home for the Nordic people. One of the main purposes of his play is to reinstall the memory of the Norse discovery of America into the minds of his audience, who will identify with the characters once they leave Scandinavia.

A play found or lost?

Larrington remarks that every fascination with Vinland and Norse 'artefacts' in America says more about contemporary ideology and historicism.[71] When Oehlenschläger wrote his Vinland play, Denmark had experienced a massive rise in population growth which lowered the living standards in the cities and challenged livelihood for farmers. Europe also experienced a record cold winter in 1829–1830 resulting in high bread prices. Civil unrests after the revolutions in 1830, followed by cholera outbreaks and potato famine in the 1840s, made America a necessary alternative for many Europeans, who now had an easier access to passenger ships due to eased travel restrictions and advancements within ship building, industry, and technology.[72] Danes, Norwegians, and Swedes left their birthplace in search for a new life, taking with them a sense of

70 Arentzen, *Literaturhistorisk*, 409.

71 Larrington, *Myths*, 252.

72 Raymond Cohn, *Mass Migration under Sail. European Immigration to the Antebellum United States* (Cambridge: Cambridge University Press, 2008), 50, 48ff, 63ff.

Scandinavian community. Old Norse literature played a crucial part in this Scandinavism which in return would influence the Vinland Sagas' status in North America. Studies reveal how amateurs and descendants of Scandinavian immigrants, especially in the Boston area and the Upper Midwest, embraced the Viking theory and attempted to replace Columbus with Leif Eriksson as the true founder of America.[73]

Oehlenschläger's *Landet fundet og forsvundet* offers a different perspective on the reception of the Vinland Sagas: It precedes many of the American adaptations of the Vinland voyages and relies more on *Eyrbyggja saga* than the more obvious Vinland Sagas. And while it celebrates the Norsemen as the true discoverers of America, it also uses the Vinland setting to stress contemporary concerns for the preservation of the Old Norse legacy and Scandinavian identity generally.

Ironically, Oehlenschläger's play has been overlooked in Danish literary history and remains unknown within medievalism studies. This might not have disappointed Oehlenschläger who reveals in his memoirs that he wrote the play mostly for his own amusement and did not expect much from it. In a letter to his daughter Marie on February 4th, 1846, Oehlenschläger posits that the historical elements will most likely only amuse members of Scandinavian societies.[74] Had it not been for Hans Peter Holst who heard him read the first act and made the director for the Danish Royal Theatre aware of it, *Landet fundet og forsvundet* might never have been performed.[75] The posthumous opera inspired by the play, *De to Armringe*, was possibly a passion project for Holst who became stage director of the Danish Royal Theatre the same year as the opera's premiere. Vinland is entirely absent in the opera which centres around the love triangle and ends with Biørn accepting Thuride and Thorkild's upcoming marriage. Instead of leaving Iceland in search for Vinland, though, he travels to 'Sydens Sol' igjen, / Der, hvor jeg har min første Hæder vundet.' (the Sun of the South again, / Where I won my first Honour).[76]

The narrative changes in *De to Armringe* suggest that the Vinland Sagas had lost some of their mysticism in 1864. After the defeat in the Second Schleswig War, Danish theatre instructors and audiences perhaps shared a nostalgic longing for the Old Norse and romantic elements in Oehlenschläger's play. Indeed, the first act of *Landet fundet og forsvundet* is more reminiscent of his earlier tragedies about star-crossed lovers like *Axel og Valborg* (1810) and *Hagbarth og Signe* (1814) although these are inspired by ballads instead of Old

73 Regal, *America's Origin*, 130–133; Barraclough, "Fake-Off", 253.
74 Oehlenschläger, *Erindringer. Fierde Bind*, 265–266.
75 Liebenberg, *Bidrag*, 363.
76 Axel Grandjean, *De to Armringe. Opera i en Act efter A. Oehlenschläger* (Copenhagen: Schubothe, 1876), 5.

Norse literature. With its setting in medieval Iceland and its compelling love story, *De to Armringe* might represent some aspects of Oehlenschläger's authorship. But by omitting the second act and the Vinland voyages, the opera loses the metatextual layer which made the concept of memory in *Landet fundet og forsvundet* uniquely topical. Not only does the heroic play reflect contemporary theories about Vinland from especially Rafn; it also reveals Oehlenschläger's concern for Scandinavian heritage and identity as well as his reflections about the poet's role as a memory curator. However, as Oehlenschläger expected, *Landet fundet og forsvundet* has unfortunately fallen into oblivion.

Anders Kristian Strand
(University of Bergen)

"And what if I enwreathed my own?" Literary Tourism as Transplantation in Wordsworth's Yarrow Poems

Abstract
This article, focusing on William Wordsworth's poems about the Scottish river Yarrow, investigates the English poet's creative refashioning of the Scottish broadsheet balladry tradition. It throws light on Wordsworth's literary tourism and demonstrates how his Yarrow poems display a complex interplay between *seeing* a site, *reading* literary texts about it, and *writing* new significance onto it. The article thus argues that Wordsworth frames his literary tourism as an "enwreathing", where the wreath is a metaphor of his creative re-organization and re-collection of elements derived from literary tradition and his own experiences as a tourist. Not only elucidating the relatively early poems Wordsworth wrote about this river, I also discuss the late and rarely analyzed poem "Musings near Aquapendente, April 1837", showing how, by means of his poetics of imagination and memory, motifs from the Scottish ballads are grafted on (or "transplanted" to) a classical landscape, thereby creating "another Yarrow" in Italy.

Keywords
Wordworth' Yarrow poems, river poetry, literary tourism, imagination, Romantic temporality

One of the most interesting rivers in Wordsworth's poetry is the Scottish river Yarrow in the Borders territory. Its name appears in five longer poems written over a span of more than 30 years beginning with "Yarrow Unvisited" from 1804 all the way to the poem opening his collection *Memorials of a Tour in Italy, 1837* "Musings near Aquapendente, April 1837". In between these two come "Yarrow Visited. September 1814", "Yarrow Revisited" from 1831, and "Extempore Effusion upon the Death of James Hogg" (1835). Demonstrating a playful relationship with place, notably the locality of the Yarrow, these poems add new layers to – or put into question – what Kate Rigby has called Wordsworth's "romantic topophilia"[1], his cult-like fascination for specific places which he frames as crucial to his poetic creativity. Without doubt these rather diverse

1 Kate Rigby, "The Rediscovery of (the other) Place in European Romanticism", *European Romantic Review* vol. 12:2 (2001), 168.

poems all manifest Wordsworth's love of the Borders region, as well as his abiding interest in the tradition of Scottish balladry, but they also display an ironic distance to this tradition, and the Yarrow locality in particular. This irony expresses itself not only in the occasional indifference to the river setting that is voiced in these texts, but also in the scarcity of sustained description typical of the romantic river poem, a feature which one finds in abundance elsewhere in Wordsworth's many poems dealing with rivers (e. g. the Duddon-cycle or various sonnets on sources, streams and waterfalls).[2] Also notable about these poems is that the Yarrow to Wordsworth is an *iterative* image with an inherent meaningfulness that can be projected on or supplemented to other sites and contexts. I employ the term iterative in the double sense of 1) repetition (from Latin *iterare:* to do again): the image that Wordsworth has of the Yarrow is of something that he can, as he writes, bring with him "where'er I go" ("Yarrow Visited") and project on whatever he wishes; 2) travelling (from Latin: *iter*) since these poems inscribe themselves into a context of voyages and tourism.

Research on these poems is scarce and mostly focuses on their biographical background or the poet's well-known obsession with textual revisions, what Ronald Schleifer calls their "poetics of repetition".[3] No attention, however, has been given to Wordsworth's depictions of *literary tourism*, a phenomenon burgeoning at the turn of the century when people increasingly were captivated by the new opportunities for travel afforded by the development of better infrastructure and what eventually became a pan-European leisure network.[4] Travelling "in the footsteps of" famous authors now became increasingly popular,[5] a vogue that ultimately became a mainstay of the tourist industry with its associ-

2 See Frederic S. Colwell, *Rivermen. A Romantic Iconography of the River and the Source* (Kingston: McGill-Queens University Press,1989).

3 Ronald Schleifer, "Wordsworth's Yarrow and the Poetics of Repetition", *Modern Language Quarterly* vol. 38 no 3 (1977). Wordsworth is known for his tendency to revise his earlier poems; see Jonathan Wordsworth, "Revision as Making: *The Prelude* and its Peers" in *Romantic Revisions* ed. Robert Brinkley and Keith Hanley, (Cambridge: Cambridge University Press, 1992), 18–43. On the biographical context, see Stephen Gill, "'The Braes of Yarrow': Poetic Context and Personal Memory in Wordsworth's 'Extempore Effusion Upon the Death of James Hogg'", *The Wordsworth Circle*, Vol. 16, no.3 (1985): 120–125; Gill: "Wordsworth, Scott, and Musings near Aquapendente", *The Centennial Review* (1992), 221–230; Jill Rubinstein: "Wordsworth and 'Localised Romance': Wordsworth's Scottish Poems", *Studies in English Literature, 1500–1900* vol. 16, no.4 (1976), 579–590.

4 Cf. Hasso Spode, "Homogenisierung und Differenzierung. Zur Ambivalenz touristischer Chronotopie-Konstruktion", in *Kultur all inclusive* ed. B. Schnepel et al. (Bielefeld: Transcript Verlang, 2013), 94–114.

5 See Aaron Santesso, "The Birth of the Birthplace: Bread Street and Literary Tourism before Stratford", *ELH,* vol. 71, no 2 (2004), 377–403; Barbara Schaff, "'In the Footsteps of…' The Semiotics of Literary Tourism", *KulturPoetik,* vol. 11,2 (2011), 166–180, or Nicola Watson, *The Literary Tourist: Readers and Places in Romantic and Victorian Britain* (London, Palgrave, 2006)

ation of authors with specific places, be it "Shakespeare country", "Hardy's Wessex", "Brontë country", "Scott-land" or, in the lifetime of the poet, "Wordsworth's Lake District".[6] The concerns and affective register of Wordsworth's poetry generally come very close to values and perspectives of modern tourism (be it the cult of heritage, the quest for authenticity, and the celebration of pristine nature). In fact, Wordsworth not only presented himself as a tourist in many of his poems;[7] he also vastly contributed to the booming Lake District tourism in the Victorian age by writing a travel guide.[8] However, his Yarrow poems are not simply recording the poet's experiences during travelling, but instead shows a complex interplay between *seeing* a site, *reading* some earlier literary texts about it, and *writing* new significance onto it. Exploiting the ambivalence of Yarrow as both the name of the locality of the river[9] and as the name of a flower, Wordsworth, as we will see, frames his poetic tourism as an "enwreathing" (3, 63), where the wreath is a metaphor of his creative reorganization and recollection of elements derived from literary tradition.

This article aims to elucidate some of the key dimensions of Wordsworth's creative tourism, with particular emphasis on the first and the last of his Yarrow poems. Writing about the Yarrow, Wordsworth is not only aware of, but exploits the fact that he travels in the shadows of a host of Borders ballads,[10] and not least those published by the "Great Minstrel of the Border" (3, 469) himself, namely Walter Scott, in his anthology of broadside ballads *Minstrelsy of the Scottish*

---

6 As Ian Ousby notes, by the 1840s, the Lake District tourism was already in full swing, with Wordsworth apparently receiving 500 visitors a year at Rydal Mount (Ousby, *The Englishman's England*, 180). Even if Wordsworth himself was somewhat skeptical (see for instance his poem "The Brothers" from 1804), his own aesthetics certainly largely contributed to the phenomenon creating what John Urry calls the "Lake-District place-myth". Urry, *Consuming Places* (London: Routledge, 1995), 203. On Wordsworth's conflicted stance on tourism generally, see John Frow, "Tourism and the Semiotics of Nostalgia", *October*, vol. 57 (1991) 123–151, particularly pp. 147–150.

7 See *Descriptive Sketches*, the famous 6th book of *The Prelude*, or *Memorials of a Tour on the Continent* from 1822, *Poems Composed or Suggested During a Tour, in the Summer of 1833*, or *Memorials of a Tour in Italy, 1837.*

8 In 1810 Wordsworth published a tourist manual called *Guide to the Lakes* (he republished it later in extended form), a topographical survey over the places in Lake District. On this, see Saeko Yoshikawa, *William Wordsworth and the Invention of Tourism* (London: Routledge, 2014).

9 The connection between rivers and modern tourism might go back to John Denham's depictions of the Thames in the topographical poem *Cooper's Hill* (1642), where the Thames is said to "visit the world" and in his "flying towers" (i. e. "tours") brings several treasures back to England. According to Aaron Santesso, Denham's poem introduced the concept of "touring" (Santesso, "The Birth of the Birthplace", 379).

10 See the anonymous "Leader-Haughs and Yarrow"; William Hamilton of Bangour: "The Braes of Yarrow" (1725); John Logan: "The Braes of Yarrow" (1781); Walter Scott's "The Dowie Dens of Yarrow" and his famous *The Lay of the Last Minstrel* whose setting is at Newark Castle lying along the stream.

Border (1802–1803). Himself of Borders descent, Scott claimed these ballads were expressions of undistorted authenticity;[11] his Yarrow was a *lieu de mémoire* of untainted proper Scottishness.[12] A crucial assumption underlying the popularity of Scott's collection, and which coincided with the contemporary romantic interest in popular and oral poetry, went back to Herder's distinction between learned and bookish art poetry ("Kunstpoesie") and oral and wild nature poetry ("Naturpoesie"): The ballads were seen as the naïve voice embodied in nature, a "natura loquitur" (nature speaks) authentically expressed through the people ("das Volk") shaped and nurtured by its local soil. In Wordsworth's Yarrow poems, the case is different. With a tourist's non-native view of the river Wordsworth reclaims tourism as not merely passive consumption of the balladic tradition, but its creative estrangement. He presents himself as a "poet-tourist"[13] who not only takes pleasure in seeing and reading the site, but who appropriates and reshapes it within his own poetic idiom. Approaching the Yarrow through his poetics of imagination and memory, Wordsworth in these poems unties what he calls his inner "vision"[14] of the river from its local reality, thus enabling an operation where the image of the river is transplanted onto new surroundings. This alteration of the Yarrow myth involves the procedure I refer to as taking Yarrow out of Yarrow, e.g., repeatedly creating "where'er I go" (3, 64) "another Yarrow" (1,667): transplanting, reshaping, proliferating, disseminating, and *re-wreathing* the literary tradition. Wordsworth's touristic poetics rely on an iterative semiotics.

Re-wreathing the Balladic Tradition

In 1814 Wordsworth first visited the river Yarrow in the company of the Scottish writer James Hogg, himself hailing from the nearby Ettrick region. Wordsworth's experience seems at first to have been a disappointment. In the poem he wrote to

11 About the ballads Scott claimed: "A real old Scottish song is a cairn gorm, … a precious relic of old times, that bears the national character stamped on it–like a cameo, that shows what the national visage was in former days, before the breed was crossed" (in letter to Washington Irving, 1817, quoted in "The Ballad and History: The Case for Scott", *Folklore*, vol. 89, no.2 (1978) 229.)

12 A *lieu de mémoire* is a place or object that "by dint of human will or the work of time has become a symbolic element of the memorial heritage of any community" (Pierre Nora: "From Lieux de mémoire to Realms of Memory", Preface to *Realms of Memory: Rethinking the French Past*, p. xvii.

13 This is my adaptation of Nicola Watson's term "reader-tourist" (Watson, *The Literary Tourist,* 2006).

14 In the following I use the following edition of Wordsworth's poems: *The Poems of William Wordsworth, vol.1–3,* Jared Curtis (The Cornell Wordsworth series), reprinted as HEB: Humanities Ebooks, 2011–2012. I quote from volume I and volume III. Quotes are indicated as volume number and page number. Here: 1, 667.

memorialize the event, "Yarrow Visited, September 1814", he starts with some lines emphasizing how lacklustre and insignificant he found the riverscape. Here is the first stanza:

> And is this – Yarrow? – *This* the Stream
> Of which my fancy cherished,
> So faithfully, a waking dream?
> An image that hath perished!
> O that some Minstrel's harp were near,
> To utter notes of gladness,
> And chase this silence from the air,
> That fills my heart with sadness.
>
> ("Yarrow Visited", 3, 62)

Compared to his "waking dream" about and "image" of the riverscape, the actual river appears devoid of meaning: the river flows more beautifully in imagination than in reality. As the twelve stanzas of the poem unfold, the poet, not satisfied with having such a dull sight before his eyes, tries to transform the insignificance of the empirical site back into a balladic context or discourse, as indicated by the reference to the "Minstrel's harp", a phrase that clearly points to Walter Scott. In fact, this attempt to enhance experience by means of literature is a key tenet of literary tourism. Already Joseph Addison had in his preface to *Remarks on Several Parts of Italy* noted: "I must confess it was not one of the least entertainments that I met with in Travelling, to examine these several Descriptions, as it were, upon the Spot, and to compare the Natural Face of the Country with the Landscape that the Poets have given us of it"[15]. Addison's wish to see a place through the lens of literature informed later literary tourism. Nicola Watson speaks of the "reader-tourists" of the 18th and 19th century who, eager to visit places they had read about in poetry or fiction, wanted to re-live its excitement.[16] As Watson elucidates, "To go to a place by the light of a book is at once to declare the place inadequately meaningful without the literary signification provided by the book, and to declare the book inadequate without this specific, anxiously located referent or paratext.".[17] Literary tourism operates on the assumption that the book will give value to the landscape, while the landscape provides deeper layers of meaning to the book.

---

15 Addison, London: Tonson, 1718, unpaginated.

16 The perhaps most famous example being Alfred Lord Tennyson who, when once visiting Lyme Regis, asked his guide about one of the characters in Jane Austen's *Persuasion:* "Show me the spot where Louisa Musgrove 'fell down and was taken up lifeless'". Ian Ousby, *The Englishman's England. Taste, Travel and the Rise of Tourism* (Cambridge: Cambridge University Press, 1990) 17.

17 Watson, *The Literary Tourist*, 7. See also Barbara Schaff who notes that "tourism is a semiotic system that writes significance onto the landscape", Schaff, "In the Footsteps", 179.

Wordsworth's opening stanza makes a somewhat ironic allusion to this touristic stratagem. The apostrophe of the "Minstrel's harp" signals that from here on the riverscape will be viewed through the lens of the balladic discourse. This is manifested when some stanzas later the speaker detects along the river a "Ruin hoary! // (...) Renowned in Border story" (3, 63), an image unmistakably denoting the setting for Scott's famous *The Lay of the Last Minstrel.* In the same vein, the speaker at one point asks about the location of the "the famous Flower / Of Yarrow Vale" (3, 62), an allusion to the rose featuring in Scott's ballad "The Dowie Dens of Yarrow" (published in *Minstrelsy of the Scottish Border*) about an unhappy love triangle which had ended with one of the lovers killed and refigured as a rose growing on the braes of the river[18]. In stanza 5 the poem dwells on the effects of this ballad or "Lay", with Wordsworth's enthusiastic embracement of the river as a "witness" to their love:

> Delicious is the Lay that sings
> The haunts of happy Lovers,
> The path that leads them to the grove,
> The leafy grove that covers:
> And Pity sanctifies the Verse
> That paints, by strength of sorrow,
> The unconquerable strength of love;
> Bear witness, rueful Yarrow!
>
> ("Yarrow Visited", 3, 63)

In accordance with the balladic conception of "natura loquitur", the river is here presented as a "witness" keeping intact to posterity the content of the balladic love story. With the repetition of the word "grove" and the allusions inherent in the phrase "all paths lead to",[19] Wordsworth clearly wants us to hear "grave". The verses demonstrate one of the most salient dimensions in Wordsworth's Yarrow poems, the interconnectedness of sadness and happiness, manifested in the repeated rhyming of "Yarrow" with "sorrow". Indeed, the old ballads about Yarrow are rather sad stories – we will soon see more examples of this – but for the speaker the sorrow is made beautiful and soothing through "delicious" verse.[20] The sorrow associated with the river is thus not repulsive to him, but rather attractive. As he puts it later in the poem, the thought of Yarrow will "cheer

18 "A fairer rose did never bloom / Than now lies cropped on Yarrow". Scott, *Minstrelsy of the Scottish Border*, vol 3 (Edinburgh: Robert Cadell, 1849), 150. The same legend was thematized in the ballads by Logan and Hamilton.

19 For instance, Proverbs 14:12 and 16:25.

20 See Philippe Ariès who speaks of "romantic death", "death which is admirable in its beauty" in *Western Attitudes towards Death from the Middle Ages to the Present* (Baltimore: Johns Hopkins University Press 1974), 58.

my mind in sorrow" (3, 64), whereby he suggests that through the medium of verse something initially sad is changed into something positive.

The balladic arch topic of love is pursued in what is arguably the key stanza of the poem, namely the 9th. This is when Wordsworth surprisingly refers to himself and bringing up his own poetic craftmanship:

How sweet, on this autumnal day,
The wild-wood fruits to gather,
And on my True-love's forehead plant
A crest of blooming heather!
And what if I enwreathed my own!
'Twere no offence to reason;
The sober Hills thus deck their brows
To meet the wintry season.

("Yarrow Visited", 1, 63f)

According to Peter J. Manning, Wordsworth in his Yarrow poems "takes up Scott's manner and absorbs echoes of the form and diction of the ballad into his own intricate stanza and gravely reflective manner"[21]. Indeed, there is much that appears in these poems that recall or evoke the ballad tradition, be it the vocabulary, the verses and rhyme, or the topics. But in this stanza Wordsworth also throws a sudden and rather surprising view on himself, unexpectedly asking: "And what if I enwreathed my own?" Quite remarkably, the speaker considers that he could make another wreath, now for himself and *not* for this creature that he calls his "True-Love". This is an enigmatic phrase, since the poem elsewhere conspicuously lacks any reference to any companion or mistress whatsoever. Who is this "True-love" for whom he wants to create a "crest of blooming heather"? Is it a reminder of the love triangle of the Yarrow legend, such as it is found in Scott's ballad? Could "True-love" be the name for the balladic tradition itself? What does the poet-speaker mean by "I enwreathed my own"?

For a clarification of what "True-love" is, we must turn to Wordsworth's first poem on the river, namely "Yarrow Unvisited" from 1804. A lively and witty poem, it was written after a tour he and his sister Dorothy had made to Scotland where they had called upon Walter Scott and visited some of the Border region with him. One place, however, they had not seen, namely Yarrow, and the poem, in eight stanzas, stages a wry reflection of that missed occasion. A crucial phrase in it is "winsome marrow", which can refer to both an attractive and cheerful companion and indeed the bone marrow. This phrase, as Wordsworth explains in a note inserted on the top of the poem, is taken from another of the ballads dealing with the Yarrow, William Hamilton of Bangour's rather morbid "The Braes of Yarrow"

21 Peter J. Manning, "Cleansing the Images: Wordsworth, Rome, and the Rise of Historicism", in *Texas Studies in Literature and Language*, vol. 33, no. 2 (1991), 283.

(1725), which treats the same fatal love as Scott's "The Dovie Dens of Yarrow". Wordsworth's paratextual note reads: "See the various Poems the scene of which is led upon the banks of the Yarrow; in particular the exquisite ballad of Hamilton beginning 'Busk ye, [Make yourself ready, my translation], busk ye, my bonny, bonny bride, / busk ye, busk ye, my winsome marrow!'" (1, 665). With this note, Wordsworth places his poem into the line of the Scottish ballad heritage, asking his reader to keep a keen eye on previous ballads on the Yarrow, whereby he, of course, creates a playful intertextual frame for his own poem. His poem stages a dialogue between two travellers, the main speaker and his "winsome marrow", where the latter wants to visit the Yarrow: "Then said my '*winsome marrow*', / Whate'er betide, we'll turn aside, / And see the Braes of Yarrow." (1, 665) This is rejected by the main speaker who rather prefers travelling "downwards with the Tweed": "But we will downward with the Tweed, / Nor turn aside to Yarrow." (1, 666) This conflict between going to see the Yarrow and travelling down the Tweed dominates the whole of the poem and is an allusion to Hamilton's ballad where the suitor of the "winsome marrow" (and murderer of her lover) had urged her to forget about Yarrow, the site of her earlier amorous encounters, and to stay with him at the Tweed: "Busk ye, and lue [love, my translation] me on the banks of Tweed / And think nae mair [no more, my translation] on the Braes of Yarrow!"[22]

In Wordsworth's poem, this conflict comes to its climax in the fourth stanza when the main speaker exhorts his companion, the "winsome marrow", to forget about Yarrow:

> 'What's Yarrow but a river bare,
> That glides the dark hills under?
> There are a thousand such elsewhere
> As worthy of your wonder.'
> – Strange words they seemed of slight and scorn;
> My True-love sighed for sorrow;
> And looked me in the face, to think
> I thus could speak of Yarrow!
>
> ("Yarrow Unvisited", 1, 666)

This stanza is separated into two parts: The first dealing with the main speaker's repudiation of the Yarrow, the second with the sorrowful reaction of his companion. Looking closer, we find a play between "worthy" and "words", an inscription hinting at the poet's identity that is sometimes found in Wordsworth's poetry. Moreover, in the last line the personal pronoun "I" turns up for the first time in the poem. In fact, this claim is promoted by Ronald Schleifer who argues that these verses point to what he calls a moment of "recognition" where the poet

22 William Hamilton of Bangour, *The Poems and Songs* (Edinburgh: Stevenson, 1850), 10.

suddenly becomes aware of himself: "The poet recollects his own words after they have been spoken (…) His own speech becomes the object of his interest, and, precipitated into self-consciousness by the look of his 'True-love', he recognizes within his act of speech – he remembers – that he is a poet."[23]

With this in mind, we can better identify the poem's protagonists: The main speaker is Wordsworth, while the "winsome marrow" or "True-love" is a quotation from the balladic tradition. And not only is she a quotation, but she might even be called the Yarrow's *genius loci*, the spirit of the place, which urges the main speaker to come with it. The rhetoric of the "genius loci" according to which a specific landscape is given a voice and a face, is a recurrent element in Wordsworth's nature poetry, where, as Geoffrey Hartman notes, it often coincides with an epitaphic and elegiac function, namely as a voice from the past admonishing the poet to be specifically attentive.[24] With the "winsome marrow" in this poem something similar is achieved: As a quotation from it as well as rhyming with it ("marrow"/"Yarrow"), she is herself a part of the body, indeed the marrow of the balladic arch legend, a *pars pro toto* of that local tradition, what Wordsworth calls "localized Romance" (3, 471). By her speech and looks of "sorrow", Wordsworth is reminded of the melancholy attractiveness of the Yarrow tradition that she embodies and personifies, which he now for the first time really acknowledges or *sees.* As Schleifer noted, this can be deemed a moment of "recognition" where the poet – Wordsworth, as suggested by the "worth"/"words" signature – suddenly becomes aware of his own discursive *estrangement* of that balladic discourse.

While Wordsworth in his poem uses phrases and images from the balladic tradition, he also shows no interest in tying these words to any experiences with the real site. The speaker's companion, then, "True-love" or "localized Romance", a personification of Yarrow's balladic lore, finds this "strange". As an emblem of tourism as romance,[25] she has grown accustomed to a different sort of tourists, the ones who comes to the locality to re-experience the balladic narrative *in situ.* In probing into Wordsworth's words and facial expression, she sadly realizes that he has an altogether different relationship with the lore of which she is the guardian spirit ("And looked me in the face, to think / I thus could speak of

23 Schleifer, "Wordsworth Yarrow", 351.

24 Geoffrey H. Hartman, "Inscriptions and Romantic Nature Poetry", in *The Unremarkable Wordsworth*, University of Minnesota Press, Minneapolis 1987, pp. 31–46. These genii loci function in much the same way as the "leech-gatherer" in the poem "Resolution and Independence", a man accidently meeting the poet-speaker on the moors and whose strange presence and discourse makes him ponder in more seriousness his own life and its relationship to the past.

25 On tourism as a modern form of romance (but with no reference to Wordsworth's Yarrow poems), see Paul Westover: "William Godwin, Literary Tourism, and Necromantism", *Studies in Romanticism*, vol.48, no.2 (2009), 299–319.

Yarrow"). To her, Wordsworth's reuse of balladic phrases does not match his reluctance to anchor them in an actual visiting of the place, which to her suggests an irreverence for the authenticity and uniqueness typical of the Scottish ballad tradition.

The question concerning the Yarrow regarding both its touristic and epistemological status is pondered further in the following stanzas. In stanza seven, one of the most crucial in Wordsworth's Yarrow poems altogether, the poet declares that Yarrow is best appreciated "unseen":

> Be Yarrow stream unseen, unknown!
> It must, or we shall rue it:
> We have a vision of our own:
> Ah! why should we undo it?
> The treasured dreams of times long past,
> We'll keep them, winsome Marrow!
> For when we're there, although 'tis fair,
> 'Twill be another Yarrow!
>
> ("Yarrow Unvisited", 1, 667)

Again, we see Wordsworth privileging his imagination over reality. In stark opposition to the "winsome marrow", the personification of "localized Romance", who in the stanza above had needed to "look him in the face" to check the speaker's words, Wordsworth holds that seeing the real Yarrow would be not only a disappointment, but even would risk "undoing" the inner "vision" and the "treasured dreams". These "dreams" and "vision" are derived from the balladic tradition, interiorized narratives and sensations not actually experienced, but drawn from books, and – as Wordsworth insists – to be treasured and kept apart from any actual sighting. By claiming that going to Yarrow would risk "undoing" them, Wordsworth assumes in complete rejection of the common notion of literary tourism that external reality would have a destructive rather than beneficial impact on his estimation of the Yarrow myth.

As we saw, when Wordsworth wrote "Yarrow Visited" after his first visit to the river in 1814, his primary impression was of the sight's dullness ("O that some Minstrel's harp were near!"), and it was only after conjuring his own inner images that he was able to overcome his disappointment. His poem thus subscribes to the kind of tourism mentioned by Judith Adler in her history of sightseeing (while referring to William Beckford): "not all late Eighteenth century styles of travel centering on sightseeing involved literal vision of the scenes or objects which lay before the traveller. Early romantics often 'closed their eyes' to immediate appearances in order to better see some other reality."[26] This points to a common topic in Wordsworth's poetics generally. For him, imagination not only takes

26 Judith Adler, "Origins of Sightseeing", *Annals of Tourism Research*, vol.16 (1989), 23f.

priority over reality, but is independent of the immediate external world, or as Hillis Miller writes, "rarely has sovereignty of the mind over things been more extravagantly asserted than by Wordsworth".[27] For Wordsworth, exterior reality is often felt as disappointing, and provokes in him the wish, as Hartman notes concerning his autobiography *The Prelude*, to poetically project a "compensatory vision" which confirms the mind's freedom over reality.[28] That freedom is realized by what Wordsworth sees as the two dominant faculties of the poetic mind: Imagination and fancy. In explaining how poems are made, Wordsworth states in the "Preface" to his *Poems* from 1815, that "the conferring, the abstracting, and the modifying powers of the Imagination, immediately and mediately acting, are all brought into conjunction."[29] This means that the imagination disposes of a host of topics and images that, transformed and regrouped ("modified"), can then be projected ("conferred") on new contexts and constellations. "Imagination", according to Wordsworth both "shapes and *creates*".[30] Wordsworth in the same "Preface" also speaks of fancy, equally "creative", and which like imagination shows the mind's ability to "aggregate and to associate, to evoke and to combine". Of particular importance is how fancy consists in "calling up, connecting, or associating, at pleasure, internal images so as to complete ideal representations of absent objects".[31] According to the poet, fancy is more capricious than imagination, primarily offering emotional colour through effects that are "surprising, playful, ludicrous, amusing, tender, or pathetic".[32]

In "Yarrow Visited" both imagination and fancy are at work. As we saw, Wordsworth projects onto the river the visions of his mind, impressing his dreams on reality. This re-making, "conferring, abstracting and modifying", "creative" operation is what he refers to when he speaks of "enwreathing" ("what if I enwreathed my own?"), an operation implying the interweaving into new poetic constellations of the images that he has garnered from his reading. As we saw, he wanted to make a "crest" to his "True-love", a kind of votive gift to the actual site. But for Wordsworth this is an operation less significant than that of making a

27 J. Hillis Miller, "Wordsworth" in *The Linguistic Moment, From Wordsworth to Stevens* (Princeton University Press, Princeton 1985), 72.

28 Geoffrey Hartman, "A Poet's Progress: Wordsworth and the *Via Naturaliter Negativa*", in *The Prelude* ed. Gill Abrams and J. Wordsworth (Norton and Company: London, 1979), 605.

29 Wordsworth, *The Poems*, vol. 2, ed John Hayden (London: Penguin, 1977), 915.

30 Wordsworth, *The Poems,* 915.

31 Wordsworth, *The Poems,* 920, 912, 918. Wordsworth's use and distinction of the terms fancy and imagination is notoriously obscure. He was influenced by both W. Taylor and Coleridge. For the philosophical background, see McFarland, *Romanticism and the Forms of Ruin* (Princeton: Princeton University Press, 1981) 90–94. On the distinction in Coleridge, see Abrams, *The Mirror and the Lamp* (Oxford: OUP, 1971) 169f. In general, modern research on Wordsworth puts little emphasis on this distinction, primarily focusing on imagination.

32 Wordsworth, *The Poems,* 919.

wreath of and for “my own” (“enwreathing my own”). This wreath is made up of images that are not simply independent of reality, as were his “vision” and “treasured dreams” in “Yarrow Unvisited”. On the contrary, in “Yarrow Visited” his inner visions are stamped on the riverscape:

> I see – but not by sight alone,
> Lov’d Yarrow, have I won thee;
> A ray of Fancy still survives –
> Her sunshine plays upon thee!
>
> (“Yarrow Visited”, 3, 64)

The stanza highlights both perception and creation: the poet sees the river, but also shapes it by means of his imagination and fancy, here metaphorized as a conferring of a “sunshine” onto the riverscape, that is the light emanating from his “treasured dreams” and “vision”. In this way Wordsworth forms an image of the river that connects inner vision with exterior sight. Rather than merely “treasuring” his dreams in a kind of archive, Wordsworth now actively exploits and connects them with the present. In the poem’s last verses, this operation of enhancing the river of the river is called a “genuine image”:

> But that I know, where’er I go,
> Thy genuine image, Yarrow!
> Will dwell with me – to heighten joy,
> And cheer my mind in sorrow.
>
> (“Yarrow Visited”, 3, 64)

The images are “genuine” because they are the products of his interweaving of inner and outer reality. Making a “wreath” out of Yarrow and taking it with him, Wordsworth thus both appropriates and refashions the inherited Yarrow. Unlike the “localized Romance”, epitomizing the site in its static quality, for Wordsworth Yarrow is an iterative phenomenon, something to be brought “where’er he goes”. He even claims that the image of Yarrow will sooth his “sorrow”, thus suggesting that it forms a charm or fetish. With “sorrow” the poet points to what Aleida Assmann calls Wordsworth’s acute awareness of the “wound of time”: time as the producer of loss and ruin.[33] Remembering Yarrow, or more precisely, the Yarrow which he had not only seen, but formed through his fancy and imagination, is to Wordsworth a means with which he hopes to withstand any feeling of despondency of time’s ravaging in the future. That the image will “dwell with me”, means that it becomes part of his memory: After having stamped his “vision” and “dreams” on the riverscape, a new entity, a “genuine image”, is produced and

33 Aleida Assmann, “Die Wunde der Zeit. Wordsworth und die romantische Erinnerung”, in *Memoria. Vergessen und Erinnern,* ed. Haverkamp und Lachmann (München: Fink, 1993), 259–382.

internalized. This process is in accordance with the poet's famous definition of poetry as "spontaneous overflow of powerful feelings [...] recollected in tranquility".[34] This memorialization of the image of Yarrow is crucial to the later Yarrow poems, as we will see in the next subchapter.

As both "Yarrow Unvisited" and "Yarrow Visited" demonstrate, Wordsworth as a literary tourist relates to the Yarrow myth and its "localized Romance" in a rather independent manner. He does not let himself be dictated by his "True-love", even if, of course, he feels her attraction. In his ingenuous poetic reshaping of balladic tradition of the site, he in fact achieves something that Scott himself had called into question, its *preservation.* In the introduction to his *Minstrelsy of the Scottish Border,* Scott had declared these old ballads to be illustrative of an authentic national character since lost, and had added that due to their precarious state "the causes of the preservation of these songs have entirely ceased or are gradually decaying".[35] What Scott had in mind was what he saw as the failure of modern-day inhabitants of the Scottish Borders to uphold the oral minstrelsy of their ancestors. However, in his Yarrow poems, Wordsworth seeks a different preservation of these ballads from the one intended by Scott. Rather than celebrating the local site, his poems shape it into an iterative "genuine image" to be brought with him "where'er I go". Yarrow is no longer tied merely to a Scottish habitat, but by route of Wordsworth's poetic tourism turned mobile and flexible. That what he calls the river's "genuine image" "dwells with me" might be taken to mean that the real authority over the river and how it is represented now resides in Wordsworth. This operation could be called Wordsworth's *re-wreathing* of the tradition.

Transplanting Yarrow in Italy: Wordsworth's re-wreathing of Scott

Wordsworth wrote three more poems dealing with the Yarrow: in 1831 "Yarrow Revisited", a poem memorializing his meeting with Scott in 1831 on his second and last trip to Yarrow. A vast bulk of the poem consists in praise of Scott, the "Great Minstrel of the Border" (3, 469).[36] Then, in 1835 Wordsworth wrote "Extempore Effusion upon the Death of James Hogg" on hearing the news of the death of Hogg, a native of the Borders region and known as the "Ettrick Shep-

34 Preface to *Lyrical Ballads,* in Mason, *Lyrical Ballads* (Edinburgh: Pearson 2007), 82.

35 Quoted in Charles G. Zug III, "The Ballad Editor as Antiquary: Scott and the Minstrelsy", *Journal of the Folklore Institute*, vol 13, No.1 (1976), 599.

36 Wordsworth added a note preceding the poem claiming that it is "a memorial of a day passed with Sir Walter Scott, and other Friends visiting the Banks of the Yarrow under his guidance (...)" (3, 469).

herd". Finally, he returned, albeit briefly, to Yarrow in his long "Musings near Aquapendente", the first poem in his collection *Memorials of a Tour in Italy, 1837.*

All three poems represent a development of the Yarrow topic: It has now become a river that is first and foremost perceived, by the poet, through memory, or what in "Yarrow Revisited" he calls "memory's shadowy moonshine" (3, 472). A melancholy feeling of the passing of time becomes more prevalent, the poems more rooted in Wordsworth's own sense of ageing. Revisiting the river, Wordsworth is moreover propelled to not only pursue, but also challenge his earlier images of it. This is particularly evident in "Extempore Effusion upon the Death of James Hogg". In this poem Wordsworth mourns the death of several writers and friends in the years before: mentioned are Coleridge, Lamb, Crabbe, Felicia Hemans, but particularly central to him are the two writers who had accompanied him on his two visits to Yarrow: In 1814 with Hogg (†1835), and in 1831 together with Walter Scott (†1832).[37] Accordingly, the Yarrow is portrayed as an epitaphic river, a river giving testimony of his two dead friends, while also questioning his old notions of Yarrow as "localized Romance": "No more of old romantic sorrows, / For slaughtered Youth or love-lorn Maid! / With sharper grief is Yarrow smitten, / And Ettrick mourns with her their poet dead." (3, 724). With his two Scottish friends dead, the era of the "romantic" and popular Yarrow-cult to which both Scott and Hogg had contributed, is decidedly over. The attractive and soothing "sorrow" associated with the Yarrow myth that he had cultivated in the earlier poems, is now replaced by "sharper grief".

An important tenet of "Extempore Effusion" is memory: the poet's recollections of shared experiences with his friends which prefigure their later death. An example is Wordsworth's memories of Hampstead in the company of the poet George Crabbe who had died in 1832:

> Our haughty life is crowned with darkness,
> Like London with its own black wreath,
> On which with thee, O Crabbe! forth-looking,
> I gazed from Hampstead's breezy heath.
>
> ("Extempore Effusion", 3, 724)

Within the epitaphic context of the poem, Wordsworth's memory of his stay in Hampstead with Crabbe provides significance to the present: the London they gazed on *then* has *now* through the workings of memory become a sign, a "black wreath", which tells of Crabbe's, Scott's, Hogg's, and the others' death. Wordsworth's memory not only relies on retrospection or the attempt to understand the past in a new way, but involves a prospective activity, a "forth-looking":

37 On context, see Stephen Gill: "'The Braes of Yarrow'. Poetic Context and personal Memory in Wordsworth's 'Extempore Effusion upon the Death of James Hogg'", *The Wordsworth Circle*, vol. 16, nr 3 (1985), 120–125.

He turns to the past to make that past say something about the miserable present. Memory itself is an "enwreathing" of images of the past which become reflective of the present. This might tell us something about Wordsworth's poetics of memory. As Aleida Assmann has noted, this poetics, essential to his autobiographical work *The Prelude*, relies on the poet's stinging awareness of loss and consciousness that his own past cannot be reproduced in its original vitality and freshness. For the romantic poet, the passing of time opens as "wound", as Assmann notes. The memory is both the condition for acknowledging this wound and its compensation; i. e. a "supplement" which does not copy or reproduce the longed-for original experience, nor heals the wound of time, but might relieve it of some of its sting.[38] As a supplement (rather than a mechanical reproduction) of the original experience, the memory is to some extent independent of it, and can be freely deployed in new contexts. According to Assmann, this points to the cooperation between memory and the enwreathing operations of imagination: "Deshalb ist die romantische Erinnerung nicht Wiederherstellung, sondern ihr Ersatz. Sie ist suggestives Rankenwerk über einer manifest gewordenden Lücke, ein Supplement der poetischen Imagination" [Therefore, romantic memory is not restoration, but its replacement. It is a suggestive vine over a gap that has become manifest, a supplement to the poetic imagination.].[39]

After "Extempore Effusion", Wordsworth returned to Yarrow and its tradition one more time, in "Musings Near Aquapendente, April 1837", a poem which more than any other shows the close connection of memory and imagination. This introductory poem is also longest and arguably the most important poem in *Memorials of a Tour in Italy*, 1837, a collection recording Wordsworth's experiences as a tourist in Italy in the early Summer of 1837. A long meandering meditation on Antiquity, Christianity, secularization, and the poet's own nearing death – and very rarely analyzed[40] – it brings us, as Martha Hale Shackford noted long ago, "the distinctive note of the philosophy of a man of sixty-seven",[41] who reflects on aging, the passing of time, and memory. The poem must also be seen in terms of literary tourism. At the time, travels to Italy had a long cultural history and could be antiquarian or "interrogative",[42] or, alternatively, hailed as a means

38 Assmann, "Die Wunde der Zeit", 378.

39 Assmann, "Die Wunde der Zeit", 374. For a more comprehensive study on Wordsworth's poetics of memory, as well as a comparison with Coleridge and de Quincey, see Lis Møller: *Erindringens Poetik. William Wordsworth, S.T. Coleridge, Thomas de Quincey* (Aarhus: Aarhus University Press, 2011). At the end of this book there is a succinct English summary.

40 The poem has been seen as one of the older Wordsworth's more unsatisfying poems, with Stephen Gill laconically remarking, "the poem has few admirers" (Gill, "The Braes", 1992), 221.

41 Shackford, "Worthsworth's Italy", in PMLA, vol. 38, no.2, (1923), 252.

42 For Santesso, this means where the tourist "was required to interrogate or engage with

for northerners to discover what was routinely described as the sensuality and vitalism of the south.[43] Both dimensions are certainly relevant to Wordsworth's poem, but its most important trait lies in another strand of 19th century tourism, the sentimental cult of the dead. This topic has recently been elucidated by Paul Westover who reveals how tourists at the time literally, in his words, "travelled to meet the dead", an enterprise anchored in a "distinctly romantic 'death of the author'".[44] This is indeed a characteristic of Wordsworth's poem. Speaking about his travels in Italy, he mentions the landscapes associated with Cicero (Tusculum), with the 17th century lyric poet and writer of epitaphs Chiabrera (Savona)[45], not to forget Tasso's burial place in Rome or Virgil's tomb in Naples, and as for Horace he hopes to travel to the Sabines to "meet the shade of Horace by the side / Of his Bandusian fount" (3, 531).[46] Nicola Watson speaks of the era's "reader-tourists" who, when visiting places associated with revered authors, hankered after the extra thrill of feeling the spirit, the "presence of an absence", hanging over it.[47] Inasmuch as "tourism represents a quest for an authentic domain of being",[48] these meetings with dead authors were assumed at the time to offer the very height of authenticity.

The most important dead author in "Musings Near Aquapendente" is Walter Scott. To Wordsworth, Scott was "the Great Minstrel of the Border", "the mighty Minstrel" (3, 723) and "the Wizard of the North" (3, 526), indeed the very embodiment of the literary Yarrow tradition. However, Wordsworth's portrayal of him is rather elegiac. He was aware that his friend, whom he had known since 1804, in the last years of his life had been dogged by ill health, economic ruin, and a certain decline of his creative powers, and when the two of them had met for the last time in 1831 at Yarrow, Wordsworth had been shocked by the physical deterioration of his friend.[49] During this meeting Scott had told him that his doc-

imaginary surroundings: one gazed upon the ruins of Rome so that one might imaginatively reconstruct it" (Santesso, "The Birth of the Birthplace," 2004), 380.

43 In the late 18th century, the voyage to Italy was often used if one needed to overcome life crises. See the "Nachwort" by Albert Meier und Heide Hollmer in: Johann Gottfried Herder, *Italienische Reise* (München: dtv, 1988), 625.

44 Paul Westover, *Necromanticism. Travelling to Meet the Dead 1750–1860* (London: Palgrave Macmillan, 2012), 3.

45 Wordsworth had some decades earlier translated some of Chiabrera's epitaphs in connection with his work on the epitaphic genre, his "Essay on Epitaphs", 1810.

46 Wordsworth's reference to Horace must be deemed extremely conventional in 19th century literary tourism. Antony Lentin writes that "So many Victorians made the pilgrimage to the site of the Sabine farm that neighbouring peasants supposed that Horace was an Englishman". See Lentin, *The Odes in English Verse* (Ware: Wordsworth Classics, 1997). Wordsworth had himself translated the Bandusia ode in the 1790s.

47 Watson *The Literary Tourist*, 7.

48 Frow, "Tourism", 129.

49 In a letter he noted: "How sadly changed did I find him from the man I had seen so healthy,

tors had ordered him to go to Italy to regain his health, but as recorded by Wordsworth, Scott had shown little aptitude for this voyage, quoting "with sadness" two lines from Wordsworth's own "Yarrow Unvisited", "'When I am there, although 'tis fair, / 'Twill be another Yarrow.'" In "Musings Near Aquapendente" Wordsworth returns to this meeting and Scott's quotation, and he also adds a few but poignant lines about the misery experienced by Scott on his Italian tour. Scott had died on his trip back from Naples in 1832, and Wordsworth had been informed by one of his companions that it had not given the Border Minstrel any pleasure:

> [...] Hope was for him no friend,
> Knowledge no help; Imagination shaped
> No promise.
> [...]
> He said, 'When I am there, although 'tis fair,
> 'Twill be another Yarrow.' Prophecy
> More than fulfilled, as gay Campania's shores
> Soon witnessed [...]
>
> ("Musings near Aquapendente", 3, 526f)

To understand these verses, with their portrayal of the sad last days of Scott unable to find any stimulus in Italy, I think it is useful to point to the concept of nostalgia. The nostalgic, according to Susan Steward, seeks for a past characterized by immediacy and presence, but the problem is that "the past [he] seeks has never existed except as a narrative, and hence, always absent, that past continually threatens to reproduce itself as a felt lack"[50] Scott's "sadness" when quoting from Wordsworth's poem falls into this category: Italy as "another Yarrow" cannot, to him, compete in beauty with his longing for the real Yarrow back home. For Scott, Italy as "another Yarrow" can therefore be nothing else than a disappointment, a distorting and false image or copy of something that in his sentiment is authentic. However, to Wordsworth this problem of nostalgia does not pose itself, because from the start he had not primarily conceived of Yarrow as an authentic presence but, as we saw in "Yarrow Unvisited", as a *literary construction* made up of balladic stories or narratives. As we saw in the previous subchapter, the quoted lines had pointed to the young Wordsworth's disillusion with reality and his privileging of the imagination over actual experience, his belief in the inner "vision" and "treasured dreams" of Yarrow rather than its empirical immediacy. Wordsworth now takes up this topic in his description of Scott's Italian

gay, and hopeful, a few years before, when he said (...) 'I mean to live till I am *eighty*, and shall write as long as I live'" (quoted in Rubinstein, "Wordsworth", 580).

50 Susan Stewart, *On Longing. Narratives of the Miniature, the Gigantic, the Souvenir, the Collection* (Durham: Duke University Press, 1993), 23.

sojourn. As he presents it, Scott had not been able to confer on the Italian scenery the inner "vision" of Yarrow in the way Wordsworth had done it in "Yarrow Visited", where he had impressed on the river a "wreath" of his inner dreams. In Scott's case, Wordsworth underscores, his nostalgia was caused by his lack of something that he deems crucial: imagination ("Imagination shaped no promise"). Thus, Scott's attempt to engage with the Italian "bright land" had failed and instead he had merely seen its "splendours" as second-rate and insignificant in comparison to his own "native" Yarrow, a Yarrow to him inextricably tied to the Scottish balladic tradition and its native soil.

In "Musings near Aquapendente" Wordsworth contrasts Scott's miserable voyage to his own joy in Italy. Contrary to Scott's nostalgia, Wordsworth approaches Italy and Aquapendente, the name of a village and a waterfall in the Lazio region, through the means of his imagination and the supplementary activity of his memory. In this way, his relation to the Yarrow accords with his statement in "Yarrow Visited" of Yarrow as an iterative image and that "where'er I go, / Thy genuine image, Yarrow! / Will dwell with me". For far from relating to Yarrow in a passive, literal, reverential, nostalgic manner, Wordsworth now *transplants* it, thereby creating Italy as "another Yarrow", retaining the image of the old one as a "genuine image" as he confers it on another. This is not a Yarrow exclusively tied to the Scottish geographic space but a Yarrow that can be created potentially wherever he travels. Unlike Scott, the merely local and "romantic" poet, Wordsworth retains a more cosmopolitan[51], universal, and synthetic gaze, because as an outsider he is not bound by the limited, embodied view of the provincial. This gain provided by a cosmopolitan perspective Wordsworth had already raised in "Yarrow Revisited", where he had urged Scott to go to the "classical" soil of Italy to find renewed strength: "May classic Fancy, linking / With native Fancy her fresh aid, / Preserve thy heart from sinking!" (3, 470) However, as it turned out, for Scott this optimistic hope was not to come true, unlike for the tourist-poet Wordsworth. As is manifest in "Musings near Aquapendente", he, not Scott, is able to "link", as he writes, the native with the classical, Yarrow with Aquapendente.

In some metapoetic lines near the end of the poem, Wordsworth somewhat enigmatically draws a conclusion:

> [...] not in vain, under these chestnut boughs
> Reclined, shall I have yielded up my soul
> To transports from the secondary founts

51 Already Coleridge had claimed in *The Friend* that cosmopolitanism is not averse to patriotism, but "at once the Nursling and the Nurse of patriotic affection". Quoted in Esther Wohlgemut, *Romantic Cosmopolitanism* (London: Palgrave MacMillan, 2009), 2f. A view with which Wordsworth here seems to contend.

Flowing of time and place, and paid to both
Due homage.

("Musings near Aquapendente", 3, 534)

I suggest that what he means by "secondary founts" is both the Italian setting of the poem, Aquapendente, and his memory of Yarrow, both of which he has "paid homage" to. This dual perspective is indeed characteristic of the poem, with Wordsworth frequently moving between images of Italy and Britain. For instance, the "broom in flower", growing at the site from which Wordsworth contemplates the waterfall named Aquapendente, is a parallel to the homely Yarrow: "She [the broom] bids me to fly to greet / Her sisters, soon like her to be attired / With golden blossoms opening at the feet / Of my own Fairfield". Having in his mind returned home and there being strengthened by a renewed vision of his homely soil – "The glad greeting given, / Given with a voice and by a look returned / Of old comradeship" (3, 525) – he can once more return to Italy and stamp his inner vision on the landscape of the Apennine. The poet "roves" (3, 527) in his imagination between the native and the Italian. These "transports" are founded on his creative memory: The term "secondary founts" might be a nod to John Locke, a philosopher clearly important to Wordsworth, who had spoken of recollections as "secondary perceptions".[52] With an intriguing change, Wordsworth calls his memories "founts", thus emphasizing that the memory of Yarrow is a source that keeps on giving, indeed enabling him through the creative and imaginative activity to see the waterfall Aquapendente as "another Yarrow".

A similar iterative conception can be detected in another metapoetical passage in the poem:

Chiefly let me cull with care
Those images of genial beauty, oft
Too lovely to be pensive in themselves
But by reflexion made so, which do best
And fitliest serve to crown with fragrant wreaths
Life's cup when almost filled with years, like mine.

("Musings near Aquapendente", 3, 530)

Wordsworth speaks of images that are made "pensive" by route of reflection, and I suggest that "pensiveness" – a term that also appears in crucial verses in the earlier Yarrow poems[53] – is exactly the word Wordsworth chooses as fitting his experiences as a literary tourist. The images are "pensive" not because the sites

52 Locke notes: "The mind has a power to revive perceptions, which it once had, with this additional perception annexed to them, that it has had them before". See Locke, *An Essay concerning Human Understanding* (Oxford: Clarendon Press 1975), 150ff.

53 In "Yarrow Visited" the speaker, looking at the river, is "not unwilling here to admit / A pensive recollection".

offered to the Wordsworthian tourist are particularly semantically potent in themselves, but because they are, in his mind, linked to images produced by the reading of literary texts about those places, images that have become "treasured dreams" ("Yarrow Unvisited"). Summoned by his imagination – what he here calls "reflexion" – these images are ready to be reused, translated, and made into, as Wordsworth importantly notes, "fragrant wreaths". This parallels my earlier claim about Wordsworth's suggestion that his poetry consists of "wreaths" made of elements from the balladic tradition. Here the site is no longer Yarrow in Scotland but "another Yarrow" in Italy, namely Aquapendente, the name for both a village and a waterfall, and which not only points to "falling water", but also to pensiveness as such, "pendente" being of the same root.

As we have seen, to Wordsworth's variant of the literary tourist, travelling implies culling images and enwreathing. This means, firstly, that touristic travel involves the collecting of images and signs[54], and these are, by the poet-tourist, made into a wreath. Secondly, in the Yarrow-poems this wreathing takes on a further meaning in that the Yarrow is also a flower growing at the riverbank, which clearly is alluded to by the frequent references to plants and planting in these poems. Taking the Yarrow out of the Yarrow, then, implies not only imposing a book-derived river-image on other rivers and landscapes, it also is an action that extends to the flower yarrow. As I have argued, the conferring of the imagination of the image on another image corresponds to the activity of "enwreathing". Thirdly, by the frequent use of this metaphor Wordsworth inscribes his Yarrow-poems into the popular notion of a poetry collection as a garland, which like the anthology or florilegium, both meaning flower-gathering, posits a metaphorical link between flowers and poems. Finally, this poetic "wreath" that "crowns" what Wordsworth calls "Life's cup" also points to *fame:* the wreath given to great authors. In the same poem he speaks of Virgil's "laurel-shaded tomb" (3, 532), evoking the plant that such wreaths are emblematically made up of. This, together with his description of his poem as a "shrine" (3, 534), underscores the meaning of the term "Life's cup" as *urn.* The wreath thus becomes a figure of his posthumous fame. This, too, plays into the contemporary notions of tourism with (as Westover claims) its "distinctly Romantic 'death of the author'" where "literary artists had to die in order to achieve 'classic' status"[55], as well as the general so-called "culture of posterity" favoured by the Romantics, i. e. their wish to survive their own death.[56] In fact, this was a crucial dimension for Wordsworth who, as

54 As John Urry noted, "The touristic gaze is constructed through signs, and tourism involves the collection of signs". Urry, *The Tourist Gaze* (London: Sage 2002), 2.

55 Westover "*Necromanticism*", 92.

56 Andrew Bennett, *Romantic Poets and the Culture of Posterity* (Cambridge: CUP, 1999). See also Hazlitt's statement: "Fame is the recompense not of the living, but of the dead. The temple of fame stands upon the grave: the flame that burns upon its altars is kindled from the

Paul de Man noted, "is one of the few poets who can write proleptically about their own death and speak, as it were, from beyond their own graves".[57] In the poem, one of the last he ever wrote, Wordsworth thus suggests that Aquapendente will be a site to be visited by future "reader-tourists" eager to meet with his own "shade", like Horace's in the Sabines. Wordsworth envisages himself as a future "genius loci" of Aquapendente.

Conclusion: "Another Yarrow"

In a letter to Allan Cunningham from 1825, Wordsworth speaks about his "indebtedness" to "the North" and the vast array of Borders literature. He mentions several important poets, including Walter Scott, and admits how much they have influenced him, but then he also adds: "Do not say that I ought to have been a Scotchman. Tear me not from the Country of Chaucer, Spenser, Shakespeare and Milton". The paragraph concludes with the following statement: "It is enough for me to be ranked in this catalogue (of writers of the Borders), and to know that I have touched the hearts of many by subjects suggested to me on Scottish ground."[58]

To "touch hearts", but not necessarily to be himself native of the "ground": for Wordsworth, as we have seen, literary tourism is a kind of both imaginative conferring of inner "visions" on new sites, and the transportation and transplantation of Yarrow out of its original habitat, thereby connecting the local with the universal. As I have tried to demonstrate, literary tourism is for Wordsworth a springboard for creativity, in which there arises a complex interplay between visiting sites, reading about them, and writing – or *rewreathing* them – anew. In Wordsworth's Yarrow poems we see an English poet-tourist who with a perspective combining distance and identification, empathy and alienation, both engages with and subverts, both visits, revisits, rewrites, and rewreathes the balladic tradition.

ashes of great men". Hazlitt, "On the living poets", in *The Complete Works of William Hazlitt vol. 5,* ed. Hove (London: Dent, 1930–1934), 143–144.

57 Paul de Man, "The Rhetoric of Temporality", in *Blindness and Insight* (London: Routledge, 1983), 225.

58 Wordsworth, "*Letters of William Wordsworth*", 230f.

Edward Payne
(Aarhus University)

Ribera, Gautier, and the French Taste for Violent Painting

Abstract

Paintings by the Spanish baroque artist Jusepe de Ribera (1591–1652) prompted a range of contradictory responses in the nineteenth century. Poets, travel writers, critics, and artists reacted to his work, especially his striking depictions of violent subjects, with both admiration and displeasure. In 1845, Théophile Gautier published a collection of poems, including two on Ribera in which he provocatively addresses the artist as 'le noir Valencian' (the black Valencian) and 'plus dur que Jupiter' (harsher than Jupiter). Through a comparative study of Ribera's paintings and Gautier's poems, this essay provides a more nuanced account of Ribera's reception during this period. The essay argues for the significance of these poetic responses by suggesting that Gautier calls attention to the problematic relationship between art making and bodily unmaking: a tension which is central to an understanding of Ribera's violent imagery, and to the myth making of Ribera as a 'violent' artist.

Keywords

Baroque Spain; romantic poetry; violence; reception; historiography

On May 5th, 1840, the French poet Théophile Gautier (1811–1872) embarked with his friend and travel companion Eugène Piot (1812–1890) on the first of his five journeys to Spain.[1] During the nineteenth century, the Iberian Peninsula was a region whose geography, history, art, and people captured the French romantic

This essay builds on my previous Ribera research, notably the exhibition and publication *Ribera: Art of Violence*, exh. cat. (London: Dulwich Picture Gallery, 2018). Earlier versions were presented at the University of London Institute in Paris, the Association of Art Historians Annual Conference in Glasgow, the French Research Seminar Series at Durham University, and the Centre for Nineteenth-Century Studies at Aarhus University. I am grateful to the participants for their invaluable feedback, and I extend special thanks to Costanza Beltrami, Frédérique Desbuissons, Lis Møller, Sebastian Ørtoft Rasmussen, and Tom Wynn. Unless otherwise noted, all translations are my own.

1 Gautier returned to Spain in 1846, 1849, 1856, and 1864. The intention of his initial trip with Piot, an art and antiquities specialist, was to purchase inexpensive artworks. For a comprehensive record of Gautier's life and works, and a critical bibliography, see theophilegautier.fr.

imagination.[2] Gautier's initial five-month tour prompted his publication of a series of travel writings and a collection of poems entitled *España*.[3] The forty-three poems range in subject from places he visited to paintings he admired, and two of them are dedicated to the Spanish baroque artist Jusepe de Ribera (1591–1652).[4] One is a longer poem of twenty-one tercets in terza rima, which he pithily entitles *Ribeira* (see below); the other is a sonnet – *Sur le Prométhée du musée de Madrid* (On the Prometheus in the Madrid Museum) – which, in fact, refers to Ribera's 1632 painting of *Tityus* in the Museo del Prado (fig. 1).[5]

SUR LE PROMÉTHÉE DU MUSÉE DE MADRID

Hélas ! il est cloué sur les croix du Caucase,
Le Titan qui, pour nous, dévalisa les cieux !
Du haut de son calvaire il insulte les dieux,
Raillant l'Olympien dont la foudre l'écrase.

Mais du moins, vers le soir, s'accoudant à la base
Du rocher où se tord le grand audacieux,
Les nymphes de la mer, des larmes dans les yeux,
Échangent avec lui quelque plaintive phrase.

Toi, cruel Ribeira, plus dur que Jupiter,
Tu fais de ses flancs creux, par d'affreuses entailles,
Couler à flots de sang des cascades d'entrailles !

2 For the impact of Spanish art on French romanticism, see Ilse Hempel Lipschutz, *Spanish Painting and the French Romantics* (Cambridge, MA: Harvard University Press, 1972) and Ilse Hempel Lipschutz, "Goya and the French Romantics" in *Manet/Velázquez: The French Taste for Spanish Painting*, ed. Gary Tinterow and Geneviève Lacambre, exh. cat. (New York: The Metropolitan Museum of Art, 2003), 161–73.

3 Gautier's travel diary, originally published as *Tra los montes* (1843), was later reissued as *Voyage en Espagne* (1845). Composed between 1839 and 1845, the poems were first published individually and then collected in a single volume, *España* (1845). On Gautier's travels in Spain, see Jacqueline Berben, "The Romantic Traveler as Questing Hero: Théophile Gautier's *Voyage en Espagne*," *Texas Studies in Literature and Language* 25, no. 3 (Fall 1983): 367–89. For a study of *España* in English, see Kathleen Koestler, *Théophile Gautier's* España (Birmingham, AL: Summa Publications, 2002), and for the most recent critical edition, see Théophile Gautier, *Œuvres poétiques complètes*, ed. Michel Brix (Paris: Bartillat, 2021).

4 For an overview of Ribera's reception, see Pierre Rosenberg, "De Ribera a Ribot. Del naturalismo al academicismo: el destino de un pintor en pos de su nacionalidad y de su definición estilística" in *Jusepe de Ribera, 1591–1652*, ed. Alfonso E. Pérez Sánchez and Nicola Spinosa, exh. cat. (Madrid: Museo Nacional del Prado, 1992), 147–63. On the reception of Ribera in eighteenth- and nineteenth-century Britain and Ireland, see Nigel Glendinning, "The 'Terrible Sublime': Ribera in Britain and Ireland" in *Spanish Art in Britain and Ireland, 1750–1920: Studies in Reception in Memory of Enriqueta Harris Frankfort*, ed. Nigel Glendinning and Hilary Macartney (Woodbridge: Tamesis, 2010), 188–97.

5 Gautier originally published *Sur le Prométhée du musée de Madrid* in 1843 and *Ribeira* in 1844. For the corrected reference to *Tityus*, see Elizabeth du Gué Trapier, *Ribera* (New York: The Hispanic Society of America, 1952), 271.

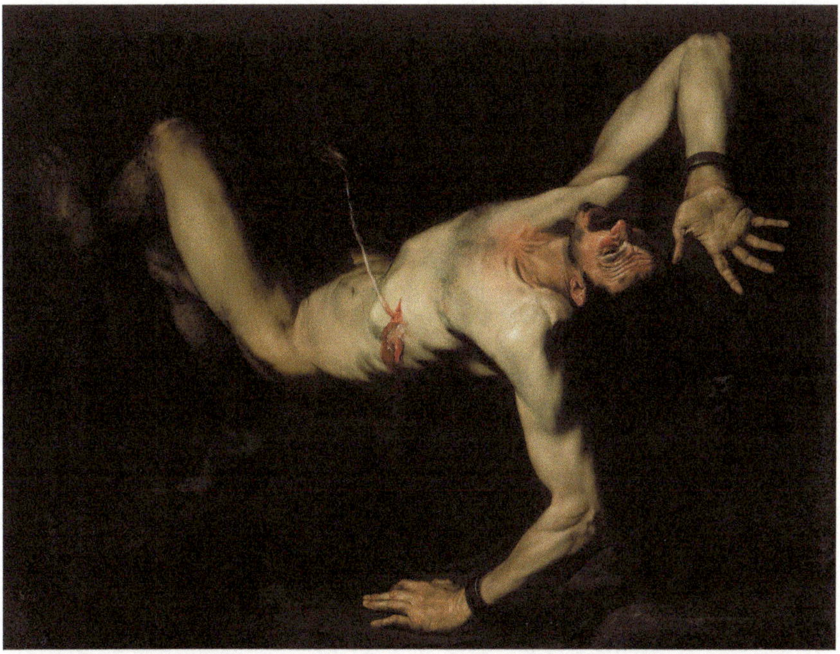

Figure 1. Jusepe de Ribera, *Tityus*, 1632. Oil on canvas, 227 x 301 cm (P001113), Museo Nacional del Prado, Madrid. Photo: © Photographic Archive Museo Nacional del Prado.

Et tu chasses le chœur des filles de la mer ;
Et tu laisses hurler, seul dans l'ombre profonde,
Le sublime voleur de la flamme féconde ![6]

ON THE PROMETHEUS IN THE MADRID MUSEUM

Alas! He is nailed to the crosses of the Caucasus,
The Titan who robbed the skies for us!
From the summit of his calvary, he insults the gods,
Taunting the Olympian whose lightning crushes him.

But at least, towards evening, leaning on the base
Of the rock where the audacious giant writhes,
Sea nymphs, with tears in their eyes,
Exchange with him some mournful phrase.

6 Théophile Gautier, *Voyage en Espagne* suivi de *España* (Paris: Éditions Gallimard, 1981 [1845]), 471.

You, cruel Ribeira, harsher than Jupiter,
From his hollow sides you make flow in streams of blood,
By way of horrible cuts, cascades of intestines![7]

And you drive away the sea daughters' songs;
And you let howl, alone in the deep shadow,
The sublime thief of the fruitful flame!

The bloody imagery of Gautier's sonnet echoes a colourful stanza from *Don Juan*, written in 1823 by Lord Byron (1788–1824), who was a touchstone writer for the French romantic poets. In the thirteenth canto, Byron describes a picture gallery at Norman Abbey:

But ever and anon to soothe your vision,
Fatigued with these hereditary glories,
There rose a Carlo Dolce or a Titian
Or wilder group of savage Salvatore's.
Here danced Albano's boys, and here the sea shone
In Vernet's ocean lights, and there the stories
Of martyrs awed, as Spagnoletto tainted
His brush with all the blood of all the sainted.[8]

'Spagnoletto', or 'the little Spaniard', refers to the nickname given to Ribera in Italy, for he spent most of his career in Naples, a Spanish possession in the seventeenth century. On the one hand, the verses of Byron and Gautier often resonate – rather uncritically – in the scholarly literature. For example, in his book on Golden Age Spain, the Catalan art historian Joan Sureda writes that the 'brushes and chisels of painters and sculptors became stained with the blood of the flayed, decapitated bodies, raised up to be crucified and transfixed by arrows'.[9] On the other hand, some scholars have swiftly dismissed the romantic poets in favour of a more rounded view of Ribera's work, which encompasses subjects ranging from Madonnas in glory to martyrs in pain. The Spanish art historian Alfonso Pérez Sánchez states that 'the irruption of Romanticism would muddy for many years the image of the great and pure painter, giving rise to the horrific artist propagated by

7 For the English translation of the first tercet, see Harald Hendrix, "The Repulsive Body: Images of Torture in Seventeenth-Century Naples" in *Bodily Extremities: Preoccupations with the Human Body in Early Modern European Culture*, ed. Florike Egmond and Robert Zwijnenberg (Aldershot: Ashgate Publishing, 2003), 71.

8 Lord Byron, *Don Juan*, xiii, 71. The final two lines concerning Ribera were translated into French by 1837: 'Byron a dit qu'il colorait ses toiles avec le sang des martyrs'. See Henri Blaze de Bury, "La Galerie espagnole au Louvre," *Revue des deux mondes* 4, no. 10 (May 15, 1837): 537.

9 Joan Sureda, *The Golden Age of Spain: Painting, Sculpture, Architecture* (New York: Vendome Press, 2008), 160.

Byron and Gautier'.[10] The Ribera specialist Gabriele Finaldi concurs that '"the black legend" of Ribera [...] owes its success and longevity largely to the resounding and memorable verses of Byron and Gautier', and he believes that it is 'undoubtedly correct to refute it', thereby drawing our attention to other aspects of the painter's oeuvre.[11] The result, however, is a rather unnuanced account of the romantic poets' rich responses to Ribera's violent imagery.

Knowledge of the artist's wider production was somewhat restricted in the nineteenth century. However, thanks to his Italian connection, Ribera was perhaps better known in France than his contemporaries Diego Velázquez (1599–1660), Bartolomé Esteban Murillo (c. 1617–1682), and Francisco de Zurbarán (1598–1664), for those who journeyed south could view works by Ribera in Rome and Naples as well as in Spain.[12] Italy was a typical stop on the Grand Tour, while Spain remained a less-travelled territory. Moreover, Ribera's work as a graphic artist was widely disseminated across Europe through the eighteen prints he produced during his career.[13] However, access to his paintings was more limited to trips abroad and visiting private collections in France before the opening of King Louis-Philippe's (1773–1850) Galerie Espagnole at the Louvre in 1838.[14] For example, Ribera's *Immaculate Conception* (fig. 2) in Salamanca was probably not so well known to a nineteenth-century French public, whereas his *Martyrdom of Saint Bartholomew* (fig. 3), now in Barcelona, was on view for over a decade at the Galerie Espagnole.

10 Alfonso E. Pérez Sánchez, "Ribera and Spain: His Spanish Patrons in Italy and Spain; The Influence of His Work on Spanish Artists" in *Jusepe de Ribera, 1591–1652*, ed. Alfonso E. Pérez Sánchez and Nicola Spinosa, exh. cat. (New York: The Metropolitan Museum of Art, 1992), 48.

11 Gabriele Finaldi, "Aspects of the Life and Work of Jusepe de Ribera, 1591–1652" (PhD thesis, The Courtauld Institute of Art, University of London, 1995), 265; Gabriele Finaldi, "Dibujos inéditos y otros poco conocidos de Jusepe de Ribera," *Boletín del Museo del Prado* 23, no. 41 (2005): 30; and Gabriele Finaldi, "Jusepe de Ribera: The Iconography of Pain in His Drawings" in *Le Dessin napolitain*, ed. Francesco Solinas and Sebastian Schütze (Rome: De Luca Editori d'Arte, 2010), 80.

12 For William Stirling, 'Ribera – the "Spagnoletto" and favourite of Naples – whose passion for the horrible was little likely to produce a favourable impression of Spanish taste, was long the sole Spaniard whose name and works were familiar to Europe'. See William Stirling, *Annals of the Artists of Spain*, vol. 1 (London: John Ollivier, 1848), 47.

13 Jonathan Brown, "Jusepe de Ribera as Printmaker" in Pérez Sánchez and Spinosa, *Jusepe de Ribera*, New York, 167–73.

14 Marshal Soult's collection on Rue de l'Université in Paris comprised the most important display of Spanish painting in France before the Galerie Espagnole (1838–48). It contained 180 Spanish works, among them paintings by Ribera, and it was frequented by artists and travellers, including the Hispanophile Richard Ford, who visited in 1816. The collection of Dr Louis La Caze, bequeathed to the Louvre in 1869, contained six paintings by Ribera, notably *The Clubfooted Boy* (1642). Sales of the Galerie Espagnole dispersed hundreds of works in England and France, some of which were acquired by provincial museums in Grenoble, Lyon, Caen, and Rouen.

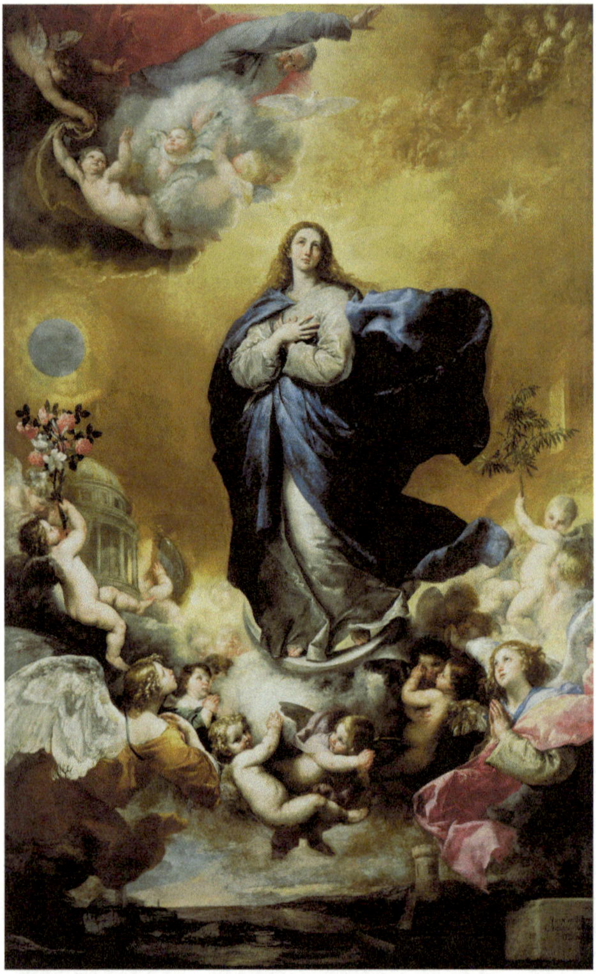

Figure 2. Jusepe de Ribera, *Immaculate Conception*, 1635. Oil on canvas, 502 x 329 cm, Convento de las Agustinas Recoletas, Salamanca. Photo: Scala, Florence.

Ribera's more violent works thus dominated the modern image of the Spanish painter. Furthermore, as we shall see, in his longer poem on Ribera, Gautier laments the absence of Apollo and Venus in the artist's oeuvre, indicating that he was unfamiliar with Ribera's more classicizing subjects, for instance his painting of *Venus and Adonis* in the Galleria Corsini, Rome.[15] According to Kathleen Koestler, these two poems, along with those dedicated to Zurbarán and the painter Juan de Valdés Leal (1622–1690), are poetic diatribes that express

15 Gautier, *Voyage en Espagne*, 472 and Trapier, *Ribera*, 271–72.

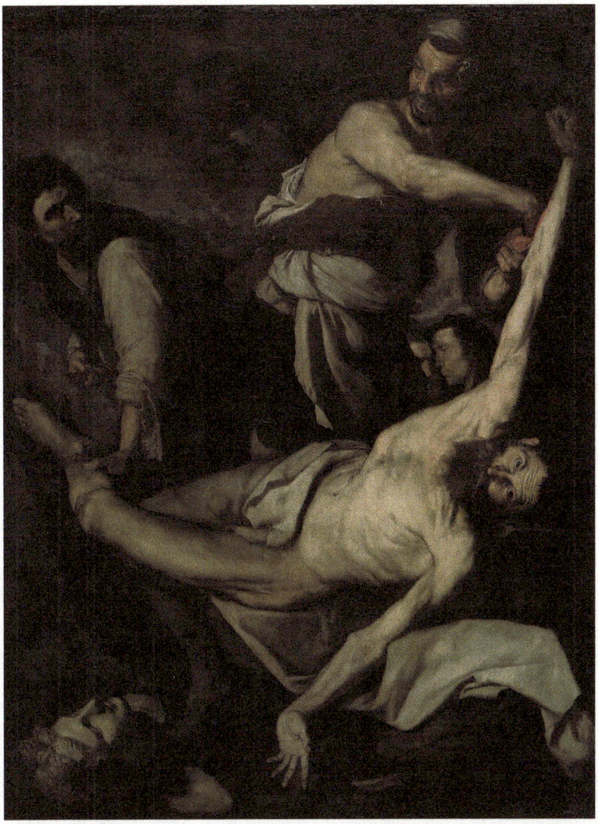

Figure 3. Jusepe de Ribera, *Martyrdom of Saint Bartholomew*, 1644. Oil on canvas, 202 x 153 cm (024162-000), MNAC. Museu Nacional d'Art de Catalunya, Barcelona. Photo: © MNAC. Museu Nacional d'Art de Catalunya, Barcelona, 2023. Calveras/Mérida/Sagristà.

Gautier's contempt for Spanish realism.[16] Nevertheless, it seems that the poet takes enormous pleasure in articulating his probing assessment of both painter and painting, thus suggesting a greater fascination for Spanish realism than has hitherto been recognized.

In this essay, I challenge the cursory treatment of the romantic poets in Ribera scholarship by arguing for the significance of these responses, which are *not*, in

16 Koestler, *Théophile Gautier's* España, 67. The issue of Gautier's relationship to realism and the realist movement has been the subject of debate, especially regarding the French painter Gustave Courbet (1819–1877). See Stéphane Guégan, "Réalisme: un rendez-vous manqué?" in *Théophile Gautier, la critique en liberté* (Paris: Réunion des musées nationaux, 1997), 59–80; Lyn Stocks, "Gautier et le réalisme," *Australian Journal of French Studies* 16, no. 3 (1999): 306–26.

fact, distorting, but revealing.[17] Just as Byron attests that Spagnoletto taints his brush with blood as opposed to paint, so, too, does Gautier directly accuse cruel Ribera of making 'flow in streams of blood, / By way of horrible cuts, cascades of intestines'. Both poets evoke an underlying tension between form and content, between the execution of the object by the hand of the artist, and the execution of the subject by the hand of the torturer. Using Gautier's poetry as a springboard for my discussion of Ribera's painting, I further suggest that Gautier emphasizes a crucial slippage in Ribera's painterly practice between artistry and artifice. By 'artistry', I refer to the material rendering of paint on canvas that collapses form into content, which, in this instance, is a fictive scene of mythological violence; by 'artifice', I refer to the pictorial device of apparently erasing the traces of art making, thus creating the illusion of 'art without art', and heightening the realism of the violence portrayed.[18] Before investigating these issues which emerge from Gautier's reading of Ribera's work, I first trace the literary and artistic origins of the subject and examine earlier models that inspired Ribera, notably the version of *Tityus* by Titian (c. 1490–1576). Then, turning to Gautier's sonnet, I analyse the opening quatrains and address Ribera's material construction of the painting's fictive subject. Finally, I explore the closing tercets and consider how Ribera's visceral, *multisensory* conception of the sinner's punishment may be interpreted as a commentary on the art of painting itself.

Ribera's *Tityus* in Context

Ribera's monumental painting *Tityus* and its pendant, *Ixion* (fig. 4), are both on display at the Prado where Gautier originally saw them. Although the hang would have changed over time, an early twentieth-century photograph suggests the setting in which Gautier would have encountered Ribera's work (fig. 5).

Looming large and dwarfing its neighbours, the painted *Tityus* must have created a dramatic impression, requiring viewers to step back and angle their gaze to take in the giant figure. Despite their enormous size, *Tityus* and *Ixion* moved around the Prado. Previously, they were displayed in a passageway at the

17 The two poems have featured more centrally in scholarship devoted to Gautier. For example, Vicki Douillet Toumayan has studied Gautier's comments on Spanish art to illuminate what they reveal about the poet himself. Refreshingly, she suggests that these insights can be useful to the art historian. Nevertheless, she concludes that Gautier's analysis of Ribera's paintings 'often misses the mark'. See Vicki Douillet Toumayan, "Théophile Gautier and Spanish Art: Figuring Duality in *España*, *Voyage en Espagne*, and Critical Writings" (PhD diss., Yale University, 2000), 10–11.

18 On the notion of 'art without art', see Sheila McTighe, *Representing from Life in Seventeenth-century Italy* (Amsterdam: Amsterdam University Press, 2020), 23–27.

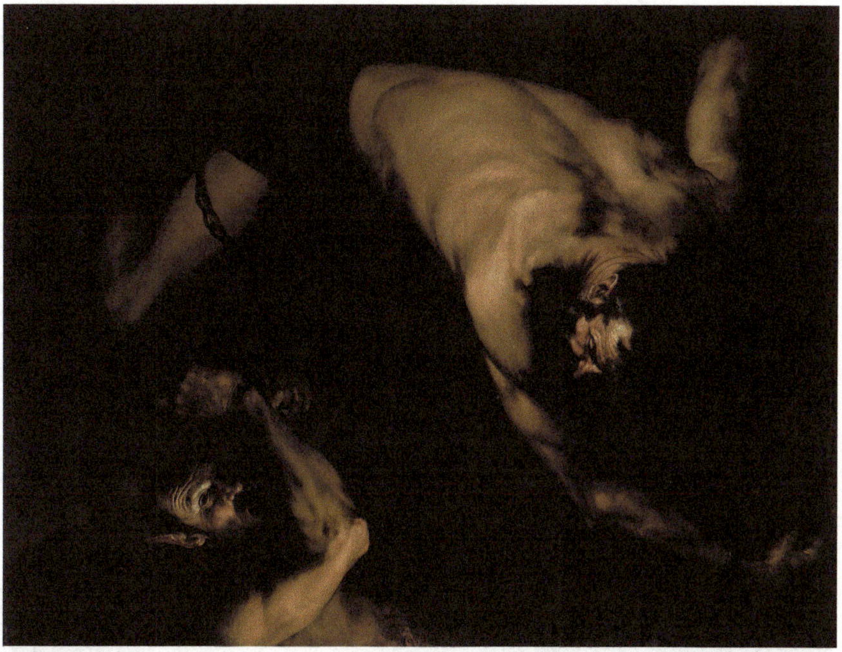

Figure 4. Jusepe de Ribera, *Ixion*, 1632. Oil on canvas, 220 x 301 cm (P001114), Museo Nacional del Prado, Madrid. Photo: Image Copyright Museo Nacional del Prado © Photo MNP / Scala, Florence.

top of a stairwell where *Ixion* was hung vertically. Now the painting hangs horizontally, its revised orientation corresponding to that of its pendant and informed by the discovery of the artist's signature on the right of the canvas.

Signed and dated 1632, *Tityus* and *Ixion* were executed at the height of the artist's career when he was resident in Naples. The two canvases no doubt formed part of a series of the so-called 'Furias', or 'Fallen Giants', which also includes the lost paintings of *Tantalus* and *Sisyphus.* In 2014, Miguel Falomir organized a remarkable exhibition at the Prado entitled *Las Furias: Alegoría política y desafío artístico* (The 'Furias': Political Allegory and Artistic Challenge), where Ribera's *Tityus* and *Ixion* were two of the major protagonists (fig. 6).[19] Artistic depictions of these subjects first emerged in the sixteenth century with Michelangelo's drawing of Tityus; the iconography was further developed in the seventeenth century, and it eventually faded out around 1700. A complete set of the 'Furias', all copies after lost originals by Ribera, is in store at the Prado, and curiously it is the only painted series of the subject that survives intact.

19 Miguel Falomir, *Las Furias: Alegoría política y desafío artístico*, exh. cat. (Madrid: Museo Nacional del Prado, 2014).

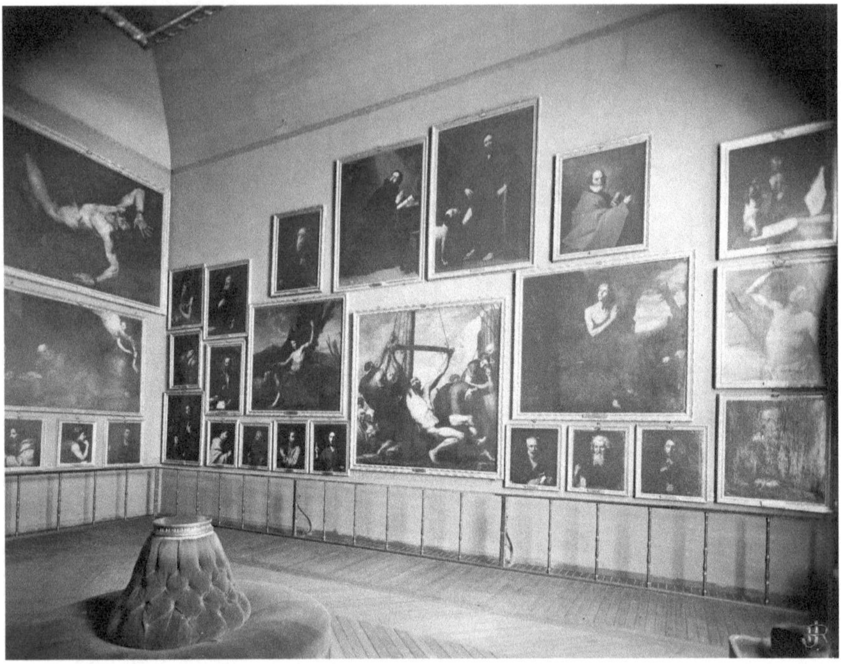

Figure 5. José Lacoste y Borde, Museo del Prado, vista de la sala de Ribera, 1907–15. Gelatin / collodion on photographic paper, 16.8 x 21.5 cm (HF01237), Museo Nacional del Prado, Madrid. Photo: © Museo Nacional del Prado.

Prior to executing the Prado paintings, Ribera depicted another version of *Tityus* that is currently in a private collection (fig. 7). Moreover, in 1633, he realized a complete set of the 'Furias', which is now lost, for the Flemish collector Lucas van Uffel (1580–1637).[20] The seventeenth-century German writer Joachim von Sandrart (1606–1688) described the terrible effects that the series had on Jacoba, Lucas's wife, who was so startled by the fingers of Ixion 'crisped with pain' that she gave birth to a child with deformed hands.[21] The Prado *Ixion*, and probably also *Tityus*, arrived in Madrid by 1634 to decorate the palace of the Buen Retiro. Indeed, the combination of the subjects and scale of the works suggests that they may have formed part of a royal commission.[22] From the late sixteenth century, artists turned to these subjects to demonstrate their skills: monumental

20 Among the paintings in van Uffel's collection was Raphael's famous portrait of Baldassare Castiglione (Musée du Louvre, Paris).

21 Joachim von Sandrart, *Academie der Bau-, Bild- und Mahlerey-Künste von 1675. Leben der berühmten Maler, Bildhauer und Baumeister* (Munich: G. Hirth Verlag, 1925 [1675]), 278. For the English translation, see Trapier, *Ribera*, 82–84.

22 Gabriele Finaldi in *Paintings for the Planet King: Philip IV and the Buen Retiro Palace*, ed. Andrés Úbeda de los Cobos, exh. cat. (Madrid: Museo Nacional del Prado, 2005), 236–37.

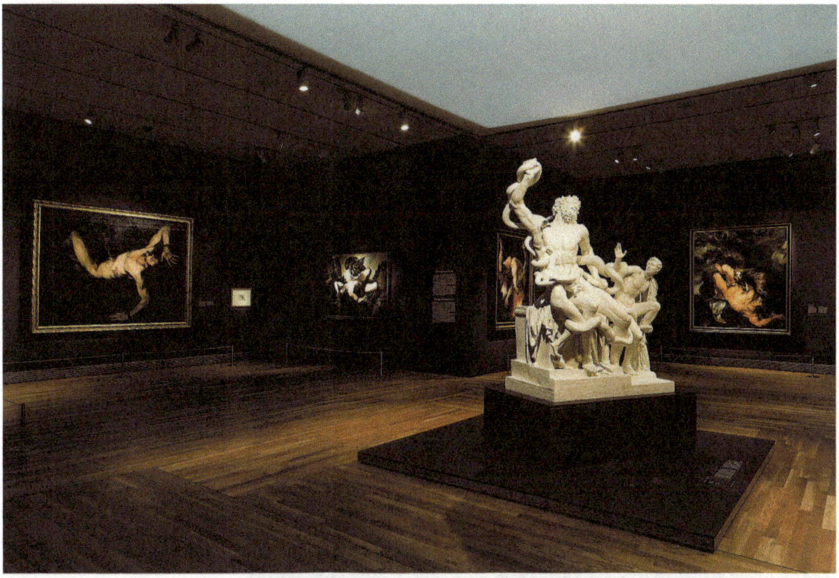

Figure 6. *Las Furias: Alegoría política y desafío artístico*, Museo Nacional del Prado, Madrid, 21 January – 4 May 2014. Photo: https://www.m-arteyculturavisual.com/2014/03/20/las-furias/.

figures in complicated positions undergoing extreme torture offered an ideal model to emulate. They are two of the largest paintings that Ribera ever made, and their common theme of physical violence is a leitmotif in his work.

Classical sources narrate the suffering of the 'Furias', sinners who had defied the gods of Olympus and were condemned to eternal punishment in the underworld. Each one had committed a different crime and suffered a distinct fate. Tityus was punished for his attempted rape of the Titaness Leto by being condemned to have a vulture visit him daily and feast upon his entrails, which then regrew overnight to provide fresh food for the bird the following day.[23] Sisyphus had betrayed Zeus/Jupiter and was condemned to carry up a hill an immense boulder that always rolled back down before he reached the summit.[24] Tantalus had served his own son as a meal for the gods and was doomed to suffer eternal hunger and thirst.[25] Ixion had attempted to rape the queen of the gods, Hera/Juno, and Zeus/Jupiter condemned him to be tied to a permanently rotating

23 For the myth and its variants, see Rainer Vollkommer, "Tityos" in *Lexicon iconographicum mythologiae classicae (LIMC)*, vol. 8, part 1 (Zurich and Dusseldorf: Artemis Verlag, 1997), 37.

24 John H. Oakley, "Sisyphos I" in *LIMC*, vol. 7, part 1 (Zurich and Munich: Artemis Verlag, 1994), 781–82.

25 There are different accounts of his crimes and punishments. See Anneliese Kossatz-Deissmann, "Tantalos" in *LIMC*, vol. 7, part 1, 839.

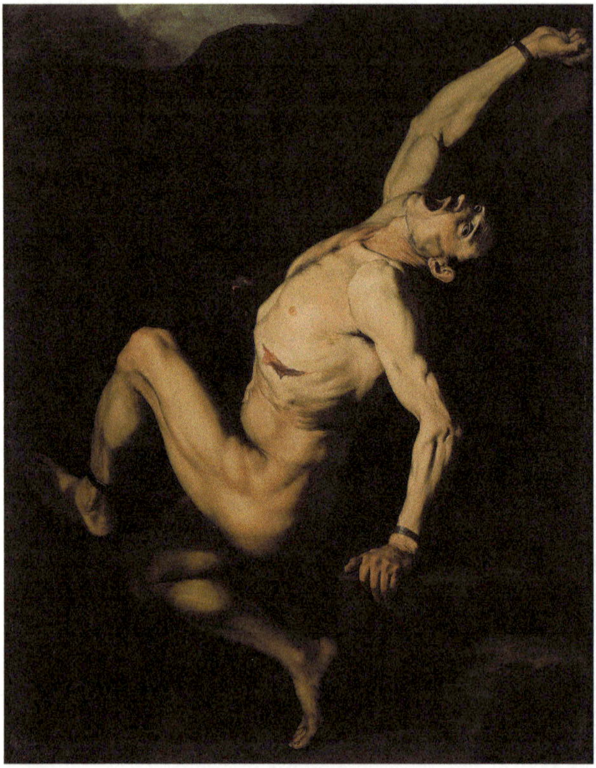

Figure 7. Jusepe de Ribera, *Tityus*, early 1620s. Oil on canvas, 193.5 x 155.5 cm, Private collection. Photo: courtesy of Sotheby's.

wheel.[26] Although he was not one of the 'Furias', Prometheus, the Titan who stole fire from Zeus, suffered a similar fate to Tityus: chained at the top of the Caucasus Mountains, he, too, was tormented daily by an eagle that fed upon his regenerating liver.[27]

Significantly, the 'Furias' appeared for the first time in the history of art as a group in 1548. This is the date of Titian's famous series of four large canvases, commissioned by Mary of Hungary (1505–1558), sister of Emperor Charles V (1500–1558), for her palace at Binche on the outskirts of Brussels. Only the painting of Sisyphus and Titian's later replica of Tityus have survived, both of which are now exhibited at the Prado (figs. 8 and 9). The 'Furias' were, in fact, associated with the German princes who had challenged Charles V and whom he had defeated the previous year in Mühlberg. At the Habsburg court, the 'Furias'

26 Catherine Lochin, "Ixion" in *LIMC*, vol. 5, part 1 (Zurich and Munich: Artemis Verlag, 1990), 857–58.

27 Jean-Robert Gisler, "Prometheus" in *LIMC*, vol. 7, part 1, 531.

were interpreted as political allegories that represented the punishment of those who dared to challenge the monarchy.[28] The term 'Furias', however, is the source of potential confusion. Originally, the 'Furias' were female characters, personifications of punishment and revenge, charged with overseeing that the fates of the condemned were carried out. But from the sixteenth century in Spain, Titian's paintings of Tityus, Sisyphus, Tantalus, and Ixion were known by this name, and ever since the word 'Furias' has been used for this subject.

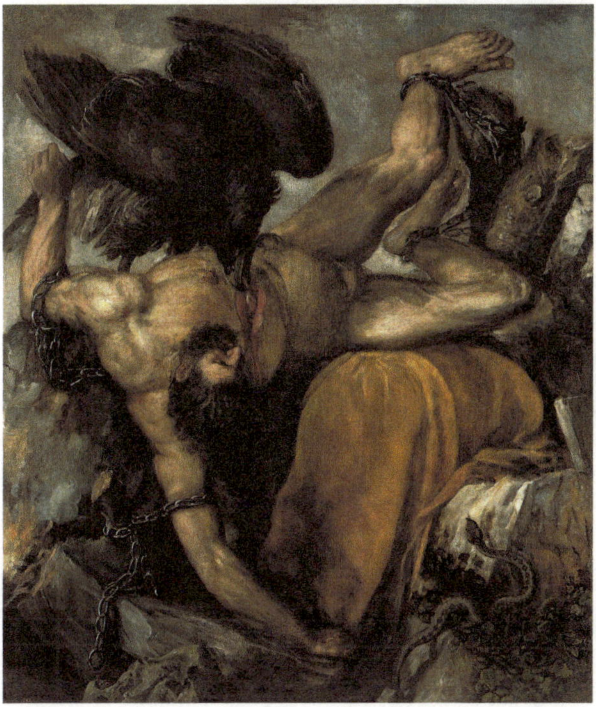

Figure 8. Titian, *Tityus*, c. 1565. Oil on canvas, 253 x 217 cm (P000427), Museo Nacional del Prado, Madrid. Photo: Image Copyright Museo Nacional del Prado © Photo MNP / Scala, Florence.

28 Pérez Sánchez, "*Ixion*" in Pérez Sánchez and Spinosa, *Jusepe de Ribera*, New York, 95. See also Thomas Puttfarken, "The Four Great Sinners" in *Titian and Tragic Painting: Aristotle's Poetics and the Rise of the Modern Artist* (New Haven and London: Yale University Press, 2005), 77–96.

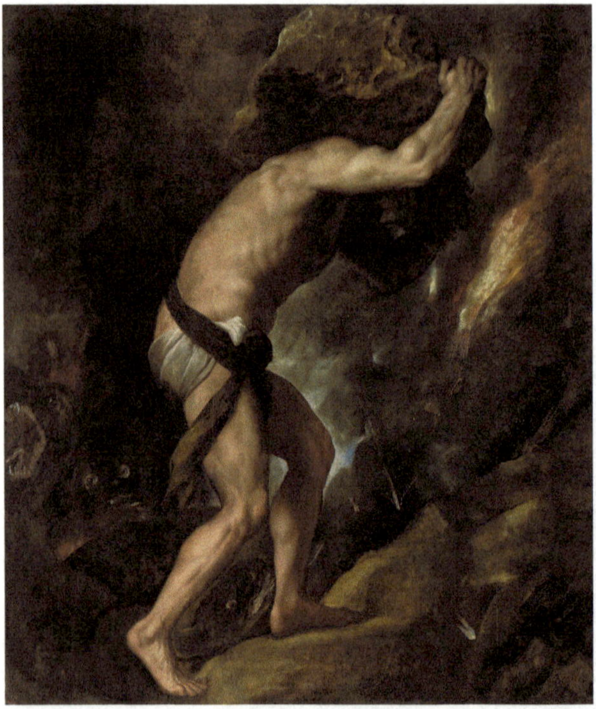

Figure 9. Titian, *Sisyphus*, 1548–49. Oil on canvas, 237 x 216 cm (P000426), Museo Nacional del Prado, Madrid. Photo: Image Copyright Museo Nacional del Prado © Photo MNP / Scala, Florence.

Artistry and the Poetics of Violence

Gautier's poem on Ribera's *Tityus* is identified as a sonnet by its length of fourteen lines, though its form is distinct from that of a Shakespearean sonnet, which is characterized by three quatrains followed by a two-line rhyming couplet. Here, the poetic construction echoes that of a Petrarchan sonnet, which is divided into an octave followed by a sestet, and Gautier marks a clear division not only in structure, but also in theme: the focus shifts dramatically from the Titan in the quatrains to the artist in the tercets. Such a notable juxtaposition – and indeed opposition – between the subject and its maker is striking. Believing that Prometheus was the protagonist of Ribera's painting, Gautier exclaims in his opening line that the Titan was chained on the Caucasus Mountains. Given their common iconographic theme, it is understandable that Gautier mistook Tityus for Prometheus, since the only feature which distinguishes the two is the bird of prey:

Prometheus was attacked by an eagle, Tityus a vulture.[29] But perhaps this was a wilful misreading, given the connections between Prometheus and artistic creation that can be traced back to classical antiquity: just as painters and sculptors fashioned human forms, so, too, did Prometheus breathe life into clay with the fire stolen from the gods.[30] Moreover, Gautier's (mis)reading may be politically charged: in the nineteenth century, the figure of Prometheus enjoyed a positive revival as a revolutionary character and benefactor of mankind.[31]

While Gautier's sonnet was prompted by his encounter with Ribera's painting, the artist's conception of Tityus may be traced back to several important sources. One of them is the Hellenistic sculpture of the *Laocoön* (fig. 10), which Ribera would have seen firsthand when he was in Rome, and which he later recorded in a drawing (fig. 11). From its rediscovery in 1506, the *Laocoön* was considered both *exemplum artis* and *exemplum doloris.*[32]

Another crucial source for Ribera's *Tityus* was the painting of the same subject by Titian. Ribera would probably have been familiar with this composition through its translation and circulation in print (figs. 12 and 13): it was initially reproduced in an engraving by Cornelis Cort (c. 1533–1578), and this printed design was subsequently copied in 1570 by Martino Rota (c. 1520–1583), who inverts Cort's already reversed composition back to the original orientation of Titian's painting. However, Ribera's image presents a radical reinvention of the subject. On a monumental size canvas, turned horizontally in contrast to Titian's vertical format, Ribera depicts the figure of Tityus in isolation, splayed across the entire picture plane and set against a dark background. The composition is considerably pared down, with all subordinate elements of the scene suppressed to sharpen the focus on the sinner's suffering body, here extremely foregrounded and starkly illuminated. Gautier translates into textual form Ribera's intimate framing of Tityus, as the giant features at the opening of the sonnet, though the first quatrain, which exposes his crimes, merely sets the stage for his punishment, which is not unveiled until the first tercet.

At the centre of both Titian and Ribera's painted compositions, catching the viewer's eye, is the vaginal wound of torture itself, blood red in the former and salmon pink in the latter.[33] While the gaping gash in Titian's painting is located in

29 Jonathan Brown, *Jusepe de Ribera: Prints and Drawings*, exh. cat. (Princeton, NJ: The Art Museum, Princeton University and Cambridge, MA: Fogg Art Museum, Harvard University, 1973), 158.

30 Falomir, *Las Furias*, 23.

31 For a cross-disciplinary study, see Caroline Corbeau-Parsons, *Prometheus in the Nineteenth Century: From Myth to Symbol* (London: Routledge, 2013).

32 Falomir, *Las Furias*, 42.

33 The vaginal form of the wound is doubly significant. It creates a striking contrast with the resolutely male subjects at work here (men writing about men who paint men), and it recalls representations of the vaginal wound of Christ, for example, in a Book of Hours made in the

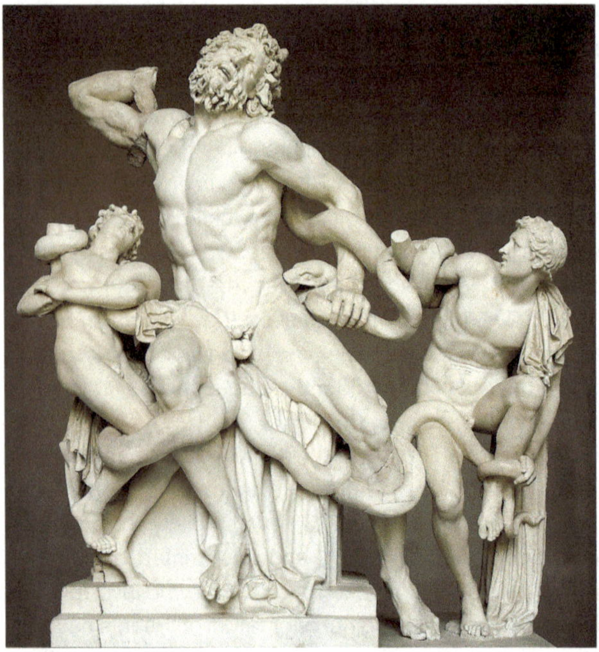

Figure 10. Attributed to Hagesandros, Athenodoros, and Polydoros of Rhodes, *Laocoön*, c. 40–30 BC. Marble, 208 x 163 x 112 cm (MV.1059.0.0), Musei Vaticani, Vatican City. Photo: Marie-Lan Nguyen (2009), Public Domain, https://commons.wikimedia.org/w/index.php?curid=1302927.

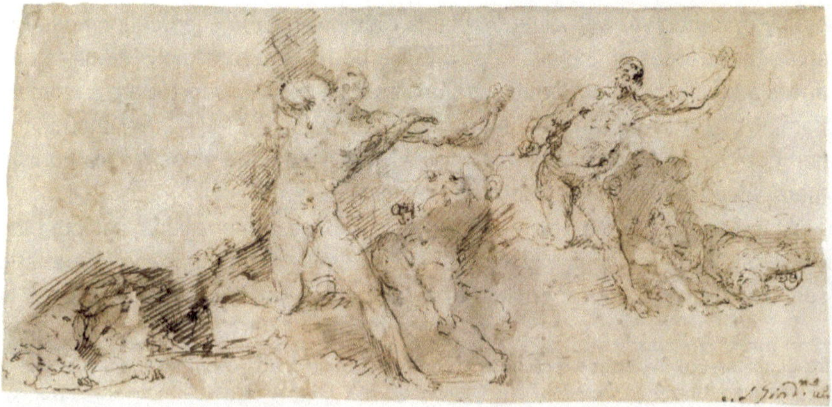

Figure 11. Jusepe de Ribera, *Studies of Laocoön*, first half of the 1630s. Pen, brown ink, and brown wash, 12.4 x 25.9 cm (F.C.125594), Istituto Centrale per la Grafica, Rome. Photo: Rome, Istituto Centrale per la Grafica, by permission of the Ministero dei Beni e delle Attività Culturali e del Turismo.

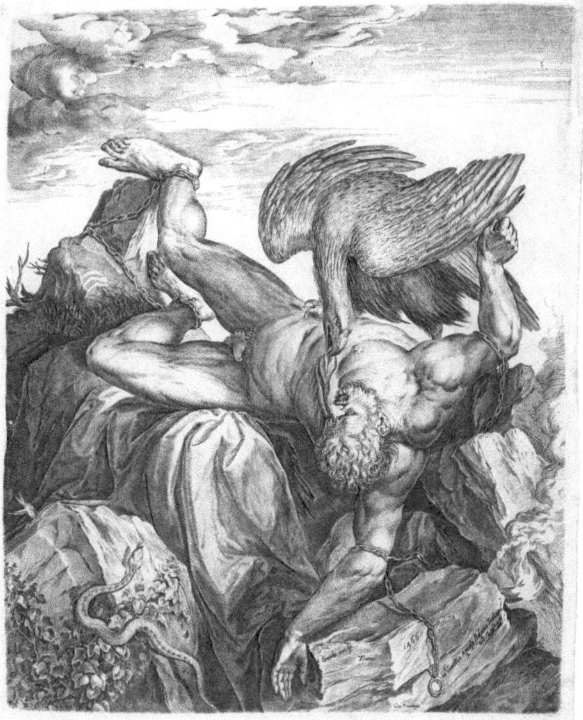

Figure 12. Cornelis Cort after Titian, *Tityus*, 1566. Engraving, 38.8 x 31.6 cm (X,1.77), The British Museum, London. Photo: © The Trustees of the British Museum. CC BY-NC-SA 4.0.

the middle of the giant's torso, the open wound in Ribera's work is on the figure's side. Despite its overtly classical subject, a Christian reference is nevertheless implicit in this painting. Though on the opposite side, the open wound on the giant's torso recalls the wound of Christ, from which flowed blood and water after he was pierced by the spear of Longinus. This practice of interweaving Christian references with classical mythology is revealed in the poem, where in the first quatrain Gautier describes Prometheus as 'cloué sur les croix du Caucase' (nailed to the crosses of the Caucasus) on 'son calvaire' (the summit of his calvary), evoking Christ's passion.[34] Moreover, Tityus's fate invites comparison

Netherlands between 1405 and 1413 (Oxford, Bodleian Library MS Lat. liturg. f. 2, fol. 4v). See Jack Hartnell, *Medieval Bodies: Life, Death and Art in the Middle Ages* (London: Wellcome Collection, 2018), 153.

34 Gautier's reference to 'les croix' in the plural is perhaps informed by Edgar Quinet's *Prométhée* (1838), which draws a parallel between Christ and Prometheus. Quinet incorrectly invokes the Fathers of the Church, notably Tertullian's expression 'crucibus Caucasorum' in *Adversus Marcionem*. See Corbeau-Parsons, *Prometheus in the Nineteenth Century*, 19–20.

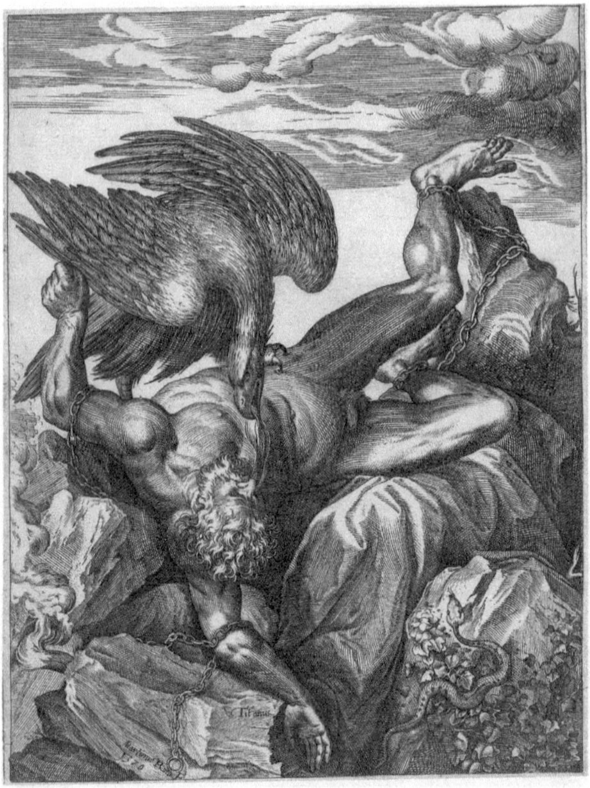

Figure 13. Martino Rota, after Cornelis Cort, after Titian, *Tityus*, 1570. Engraving, 20 x 15.5 cm (1873,0809.800), The British Museum, London. Photo: © The Trustees of the British Museum. CC BY-NC-SA 4.0.

with scenes of religious martyrdom, notably Saint Erasmus who was tortured by having his intestines extracted and wrapped around a windlass.[35] There are further parallels with Ribera's own depictions of religious violence, for example the *Martyrdom of Saint Bartholomew* (fig. 3). While the executioners in this scene are prominently presented, in *Tityus*, the torturer – a bird rather than a human – subtly blends into the encasing blackness, which may be amplified due to the pigment darkening over time. In contrast to Titian's painting, where the vulture is portrayed in full and completely dominates the victim, Ribera's focus remains on the tortured rather than the torturer.

Ribera was especially preoccupied with the tradition and challenge of representing the suffering body. However, his conception of the body in pain departs

35 For a contemporary depiction of the subject, see Nicolas Poussin, *Martyrdom of Saint Erasmus*, 1628–29. Oil on canvas, 320 x 186 cm, Musei Vaticani, Vatican City.

radically from Titian's, who evokes suffering only in the twisted position of Tityus. Ribera articulates the searing pain of the sinner's punishment both through his complicated pose and his facial expression. However, it is difficult to read the expression on the protagonist's inverted face, and we have to twist and turn our own bodies to see it right side up. By inverting Tityus's head, Ribera directs our attention to his writhing body. The painter returns to this pictorial device when he represents the torture of another mythological figure. Tityus's vulnerable body, upturned head, and screaming mouth anticipate Ribera's monumental painting of *Apollo and Marsyas* (fig. 14). After having challenged Apollo to a musical competition, Marsyas was defeated and punished for his hubris by being tied to a tree and flayed alive. In the version at the Museo di Capodimonte, Naples, Ribera represents Apollo starting to skin the satyr, whose bloodcurdling screams appal the figures at the far right.

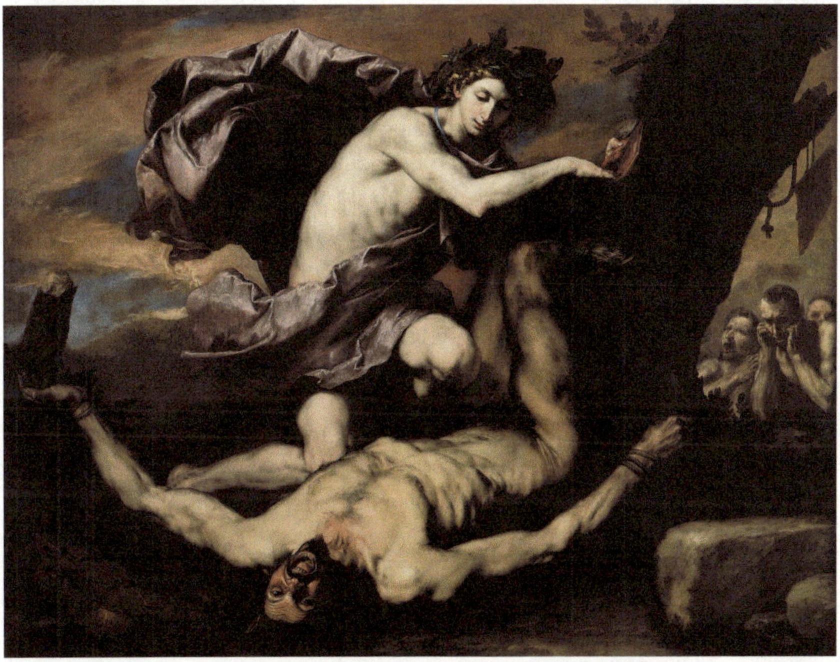

Figure 14. Jusepe de Ribera, *Apollo and Marsyas*, 1637. Oil on canvas, 182 x 232 cm (Quintavalle, 511), Museo e Real Bosco di Capodimonte, Naples. Photo: Archivio Fotografico del Polo Museale della Campania © Museo e Real Bosco di Capodimonte, by permission of the Ministero dei Beni e delle Attività Culturali e del Turismo.

Similarly, one of the most striking elements of Ribera's *Tityus* is its elaborate commentary on the *senses* of violence. This dimension of the work must have appealed to Gautier. The final line of the sonnet, where Prometheus is described as 'the sublime thief' of life-giving fire, introduces the concept of the sublime, an aesthetic sentiment characterized by the eighteenth-century Irish philosopher Edmund Burke as that which is both terrible and pleasurable, capable of arousing ideas of pain and danger, at once alluring and repelling the viewer by an overwhelming, almost threatening force.[36] For Gautier, Ribera's *Tityus* is exemplary in its provocation of the sublime: the poet contrasts the 'cruel' painter with the compassionate nymphs who temper the sublimity of violence by offering an emotional cue for the reader or viewer to respond to the scene.

Ultimately, Ribera's *Tityus* was designed to create a profound impression on the spectator through its scale, subject, and artistic construction. The allusions to the five senses transform this classical theme into a visceral event, and the violent subject matter enables Ribera to exploit his virtuosity as the painter *par excellence* of physical suffering. A multisensory portrayal, Ribera's *Tityus* transcends its mythological boundaries to evoke the physiological experience of suffering: we feel pain or at least discomfort when observing the torment of the sinner. Paradoxically, the artist has here crafted a scene that is at once painful to look at, yet difficult to turn away from.

The giant both disturbs, howling in pain as a vulture pecks his intestines with its beak, and distances the viewer through his gesturing hand. It is noteworthy that the position of Tityus's body appears to be defining the enormous dimensions of the picture and the limits of the canvas. Writhing in agony, the figure rests his left hand parallel to the painting's lower edge, while his right elbow points to the upper limit, and his left foot is adjacent to the left side. Moreover, Tityus presses the palm of his right hand against the edge of the picture plane, indicating the boundaries of the painting and effectively pushing the viewer back in space. It thus appears as if Tityus is trapped not only in the classical underworld, but also within the pictorial composition. The painting thus operates as if there were a 'fourth dimension' or transparent surface against which the figure's palm is pressing. While the painter refrains from breaking the picture plane, the poet transgresses this liminal boundary: addressing the painter ('toi, cruel Ribeira') rather than the protagonist of the painting (described in the third person), Gautier simultaneously implicates the reader or viewer, heightening the fictive nature of the underworld while both painter and poet occupy a parallel 'audience' position.

The prominence of Tityus's open right hand further alludes to the sense of touch. In the same year that he made this work, Ribera painted an allegory of touch that is also in the Prado (fig. 15). It represents a blind man holding a sculpted bust that rests on a table next to a painting of a head that the man cannot

36 Edmund Burke, *A Philosophical Enquiry into the Origin of our Ideas of the Sublime and the Beautiful* (Oxford: Oxford University Press, 1990 [1757]), 36. See also Glendinning, "Terrible Sublime," 192–93.

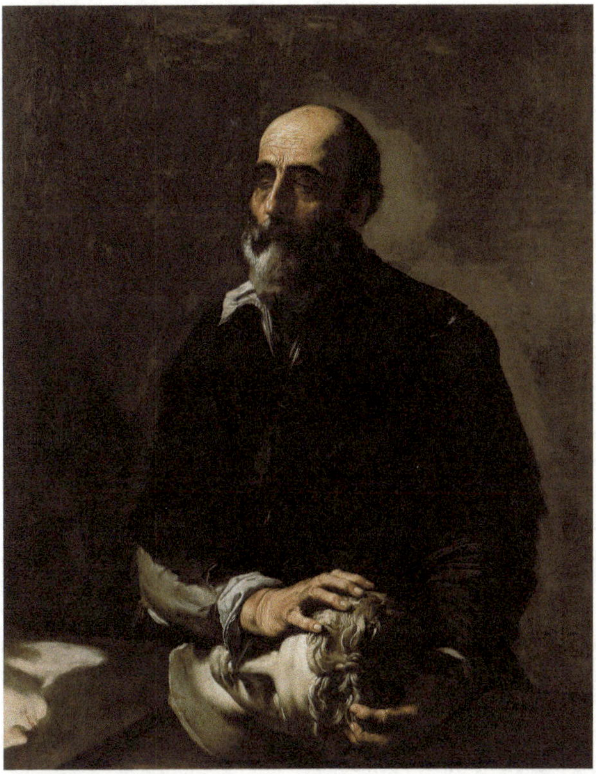

Figure 15. Jusepe de Ribera, *Sense of Touch*, 1632. Oil on canvas, 125 x 98 cm (P001112), Museo Nacional del Prado, Madrid. Photo: Image Copyright Museo Nacional del Prado © Photo MNP / Scala, Florence.

see. This juxtaposition enables Ribera to allude to the *paragone*, or competition, between sculpture and painting through their associated senses of touch and sight.

During his youth in Rome, Ribera completed a series of five paintings representing allegories of the five senses, which were a crucial preoccupation throughout his career.[37] In *Tityus*, the left hand of the figure, pressing against the hard rock at the lower edge of the canvas, sharply contrasts with the soft matter of his entrails being painfully torn out. The chained hands of Tityus recall the crimes of the giant, who sought the pleasures of touch in his attempted rape of Leto and now must suffer the pains of his own corporal violation. Perhaps the prominence of the sinner's hand can also be connected to the central role of the artist's hand, which, to invoke Elaine Scarry's terms, both 'makes' the figure and 'unmakes' the

37 For a recent interpretation of the series, see Hannah Joy Friedman, "Jusepe de Ribera's *Five Senses* and the Practice of Prudence," *Renaissance Quarterly* 74 (2021): 1111–61.

victim.[38] This striking tension between the activities of 'making and unmaking', creation and destruction, is especially fitting to the subjects of Tityus and Prometheus, whose bodies are continuously made, unmade, and remade. The vulture devouring the intestine is an explicit reference to the sense of taste, and Ribera clearly alludes to sound through the open mouth of Tityus, howling in anguish. Especially noteworthy is the attentive rendering of skin, as the flushed face and neck evoke the intensity of the giant's cries.

When considering the process of 'making' a work of art, whether a poem or a painting, we may take into account Aristotle's concept of imitation, where the artist's pleasure in representing disturbing subjects can be related to the viewer's pleasure in recognizing the content of such a depiction or, when it is not recognizable, in admiring its form:

> Speaking generally, poetry seems to owe its origin to two particular causes, both natural. From childhood men have an instinct for representation, and in this respect man differs from the other animals that he is far more imitative and learns his first lessons by representing things. And then there is the enjoyment people always get from representations. What happens in actual experience proves this, for we enjoy looking at accurate likenesses of things which are themselves painful to see, obscene beasts, for instance, and corpses. The reason is this. Learning things gives great pleasure not only to philosophers but also in the same way to all other men, though they share this pleasure only to a small degree. The reason why we enjoy seeing likenesses is that, as we look, we learn and infer what each is, for instance, "that is so and so". If we have never happened to see the original, our pleasure is not due to the representation as such but to the technique or the colour or some other such cause.[39]

This twofold power of visual mimesis is noted by Ribera's eighteenth-century Spanish biographer, Antonio Palomino (1655–1726), who refers, among other works, to his *Tityus:*

> No se deleitaba tanto Ribera en pintar cosas dulces, y devotas, como en expressar cosas horrendas, y asperas: quales son los cuerpos de los ancianos, secos, arrugados, y consumidos, con el rostro enjuto, y malicento; todo hecho puntualmente por el natural, con extremado primor, fuerza, y elegante manejo: como lo manifiesta el San Bartolomé en el Martyrio, quitandole la piel, y descubierta la Anathomia interior del brazo: el célebre Ticio, á quien el Buitre le saca las entrañas, por castigo de su insolente atrevimiento: los tormentos de Sisifo, de Tantalo, y de Ixion.[40]

38 Elaine Scarry, *The Body in Pain: The Making and Unmaking of the World* (Oxford: Oxford University Press, 1985).

39 Aristotle, *The Poetics*, trans. W. Hamilton Fyfe (London: William Heinemann and Cambridge, MA: Harvard University Press, 1946), 13–15. See also Hendrix, "The Repulsive Body," 82–83.

40 'Ribera did not enjoy painting sweet and devout subjects as much as he liked expressing horrifying and harsh things, such as the bodies of old men: dry, wrinkled, and lean, with gaunt and withered faces, everything done accurately after the model with extraordinary skill, vigor,

It is important to note how Palomino, unlike Gautier, frames Ribera in terms of *depicting* scenes of violence with skill and elegance, as opposed to cruelly *inflicting* torture himself.

Despite the graphic realism of Ribera's portrayal of *Tityus*, we are nevertheless reminded that we are looking at a painted object of a fictive subject. For example, both Titian and Ribera take more care in representing the upper half of the giant's body than they do the lower. In Titian's version, the awkwardly positioned legs are disproportionately shorter than the rest of the body, while in Ribera's they appear both out of scale with the torso – as if executed from a different model or another pose – and more loosely rendered. Ribera's artistic practice, however, did not merely concern the literal transcription of the body, but rather the calculated manipulation of the human form. Although the artist would certainly have followed the tradition of Caravaggio (1571–1610) in working after the posed model, lying on the ground, the position of this figure is undeniably difficult, if not anatomically impossible, to recreate. Ribera not only demonstrates his skill in representing the body in complicated configurations, but also articulates the body as a complex, incoherent entity, and contrasts the possibilities of painting with the limitations of human anatomy. In this instance, the artist betrays the material construction of the scene, underscoring the fictive nature of the violence portrayed, and reminding us that we are beholding the staged torment of a *figure* in a painting, as opposed to the real suffering of a *person* in agony. Ultimately, Ribera heightens the tensions between the painting's political resonance (rebels versus Habsburgs), its paradoxical realism, and its self-aware potential as a fictive construction.[41]

and elegant technique. This is manifested by the Martyrdom of Saint Bartholomew, in which he is being flayed and the internal anatomy of the arm is exposed, by the celebrated Tityus, whose entrails are being devoured by a vulture as a punishment for his wanton audacity, and by the torments of Sisyphus, Tantalus, and Ixion.' Antonio Palomino de Castro y Velasco, *El Museo pictórico y escala óptica*, III, *El Parnaso español pintoresco laureado* (Madrid: Lucas Antonio de Bedmar, 1724), 311. For the English translation, see Antonio Palomino, *Lives of the Eminent Spanish Painters and Sculptors*, trans. Nina Ayala Mallory (Cambridge: Cambridge University Press, 1987), 123.

41 In contrast, Gautier paid little attention to the political convulsions of nineteenth-century Spain. However, *Voyage en Espagne* and *España* reveal an equally complex interplay between reality, 'un-reality', and the realistic description of artworks as a fictive and a literary strategy. See Vincent Vivès, "Théophile Gautier: la traversée des apparences" in *Image et voyage: Représentations iconographiques du voyage, de la Méditerranée aux Indes orientales et occidentales, de la fin du Moyen Âge au XIXe siècle*, ed. Sylvie Requemora-Gros and Loic P. Guyon (Aix-en-Provence: Presses universitaires de Provence, 2012), 235–46. https://doi.org/10.4000/books.pup.21972.

Violence and the Artifice of Paint

Let us now consider the final tercets of Gautier's sonnet where the poet forcefully accuses the painter of inflicting actual physical pain on his subject. Unlike a Shakespearean sonnet, where the rhyming couplet presents a resolution to the problem posed in the opening quatrains, here Gautier resolves no problem, but rather problematizes both painting and poem as he abruptly shifts his focus from the fictive creation of *Tityus* to its very real creator. While the crimes of the giant are unveiled in the first part of the poem, the crimes of the artist are expressed in the second.

As mentioned above, the poet addresses the painter directly, boldly employing the informal personal pronoun 'tu' as opposed to the formal 'vous', and declaring that Ribera is 'plus dur que Jupiter' (harsher than Jupiter), the most powerful Roman god. Ribera's 'harshness' is here manifested by his concentration on the most extreme moment of the giant's ordeal. We may recall, for example, that during the night, Tityus's entrails regrew for the next day's feast. For Gautier, however, the artist has chosen to depict the heights of violence by only portraying the consumption of 'cascades d'entrailles' (cascades of intestines) rather than the sinner's restored body. Invoking the rivalrous relationship between the spatial dimension of painting versus the temporal qualities of poetry, Ribera fittingly portrays the giant on a monumental scale, suspending for all time his merciless torture. Furthermore, the presence in the poem's second quatrain of 'Les nymphes de la mer, des larmes dans les yeux' (Sea nymphs, with tears in their eyes) is in the painting nowhere to be found. Gautier's inclusion of such affective responses inevitably heightens the drama, recalling how Ribera, in such paintings as *Apollo and Marsyas* (fig. 14), incorporates 'onlookers' who compassionately witness the violent episode. In *Tityus*, however, Ribera paints compassion out of the scene, abandoning the protagonist to suffer eternally, alone, in the profound darkness of his canvas.

The 'harshness' to which Gautier refers is suggestive not only of the brutal subject matter depicted, but also of the visceral manner in which it is executed. Although the artist paints with a thick impasto, allowing the bristles of his brush to describe meticulously skin creases and individual hairs, from a distance, Ribera's apparent efforts to erase the traces of his tools create the illusion that the work was not made by human hands. The graphic realism of the violence portrayed is so raw that it is like a wound itself. Despite the figure's anatomical anomalies, the imposing dimensions of the painting pose a threat to the viewer. Indeed, the painting's address was directed at a specific audience: as previously mentioned, depictions of the 'Furias' functioned as political allegories at the Habsburg court, representing the punishment of those who dared to challenge the monarchy.

This threatening address to the spectator is further echoed in Gautier's poem, as his accusations towards Ribera simultaneously appear directed at the reader, who becomes the implied subject of the pronoun 'tu'. From the distant, fictive story of the sinner, recounted in the third person in the opening quatrains, to the dangerous proximity of the second person form of address in the final lines, Gautier here implicates us in the torture of Tityus. For the poet, the violent, repeated onslaughts of the bird parallel the actions of the painter in his role as 'torturer', yet the emphatic reiteration of the pronoun 'tu' in the tercets converts Gautier into an attacker on Ribera. However, despite the poet's accusations against the painter, his construction of the 'artist-as-executioner' is problematic, for the *painter* merely executes the *painting* and does not himself cause Tityus's pain. Perhaps Gautier, rather than Ribera, is guilty of embellishing the violence that is otherwise implied in the painting.

The poet's conception of the painter as not only a violent artist, but also himself a troubled figure, is confirmed in his longer poem *Ribeira* (see Appendix for translation):

Il est des cœurs épris du triste amour du laid.
Tu fus un de ceux-là, peintre à la rude brosse
Que Naple a salué du nom d'Espagnolet.

Rien ne put amollir ton âpreté féroce,
Et le splendide azur du ciel italien
N'a laissé nul reflet dans ta peinture atroce.

Chez toi, l'on voit toujours le noir Valencien,
Paysan hasardeux, mendiant équivoque,
More que le baptême à peine a fait chrétien.

Comme un autre le beau, tu cherches ce qui choque :
Les martyrs, les bourreaux, les *gitanos*, les gueux,
Étalant un ulcère à côté d'une loque ;

Les vieux au chef branlant, au cuir jaune et rugueux,
Versant sur quelque Bible un flot de barbe grise ;
Voilà ce qui convient à ton pinceau fougueux.

Tu ne dédaignes rien de ce que l'on méprise ;
Nul haillon, Ribeira, par toi n'est rebuté :
Le vrai, toujours le vrai, c'est ta seule devise !

Et tu sais revêtir d'une étrange beauté
Ces trois monstres abjects, effroi de l'art antique,
La Douleur, la Misère et la Caducité.

Pour toi, pas d'Apollon, pas de Vénus pudique ;
Tu n'admets pas un seul de ces beaux rêves blancs
Taillés dans le paros ou dans le pentélique.

Il te faut des sujets sombres et violents
Où l'ange des douleurs vide ses noirs calices,
Où la hache s'émousse aux billots ruisselants.

Tu sembles enivré par le vin des supplices,
Comme un César romain dans sa pourpre insulté,
Ou comme un victimaire après vingt sacrifices.

Avec quelle furie et quelle volupté
Tu retournes la peau du martyr qu'on écorche,
Pour nous en faire voir l'envers ensanglanté !

Aux pieds des patients comme tu mets la torche !
Dans le flanc de Caton comme tu fais crier
La plaie, affreuse bouche ouverte comme un porche !

D'où te vient, Ribeira, cet instinct meurtrier ?
Quelle dent t'a mordu, qui te donne la rage,
Pour tordre ainsi l'espèce humaine et la broyer ?

Que t'a donc fait le monde, et, dans tout ce carnage,
Quel ennemi secret de tes coups poursuis-tu ?
Pour tant de sang versé quel était donc l'outrage ?

Ce martyr, c'est le corps d'un rival abattu ;
Et ce n'est pas toujours au cœur de Prométhée
Que fouille l'aigle fauve avec son bec pointu.

De quelle ambition du ciel précipitée,
De quel espoir traîné par des coursiers sans frein,
Ton âme de démon était-elle agitée ?

Qu'avais-tu donc perdu pour être si chagrin ?
De quels amours tournés se composaient tes haines,
Et qui jalousais-tu, toi, peintre souverain ?

Les plus grands cœurs, hélas ! ont les plus grandes peines ;
Dans la coupe profonde il tient plus de douleurs ;
Le ciel se venge ainsi sur les gloires humaines.

Un jour, las de l'horrible et des noires couleurs,
Tu voulus peindre aussi des corps blancs comme neige,
Des anges souriants, des oiseaux et des fleurs,

Des nymphes dans les bois que le satyre assiège,
Des amours endormis sur un sein frémissant,
Et tous ces frais motifs chers au moelleux Corrège ;

Mais tu ne sus trouver que du rouge de sang,
Et quand du haut des cieux, apportant l'auréole,
Sur le front de tes saints l'ange de Dieu descend,

En détournant les yeux, il la pose et s'envole !

Here, Gautier typifies Ribera through the 'black legend' of Spain: the negative construction of the country in the propaganda of other early modern imperial powers, notably England. The artist is introduced as 'Espagnolet', the French translation of his Italian nickname 'Lo Spagnoletto', which emphasizes Ribera's Spanish origins. The poet denies the possibility of Ribera's dual identity as a migrant artist (born in Valencia but active in Spanish Naples) by arguing that he remained a 'black Valencian' under the luminous Italian sky. The idea of an essential, unchanging identity emerges even more sharply when Ribera is tainted as being 'More que le baptême à peine a fait chrétien' (a Moor that baptism hardly made a Christian). In Spain, Ribera's lifetime was marked by a growing anxiety around miscegenation and cultural hybridity, which involved the expulsion of the Moriscos (converted Muslims) in 1609–14. A reason for such anxiety was the fact that Muslims (and converted Muslims) could not readily be identified by physical appearance, leading to attempts to police cultural and religious expressions and generating an obsession for 'purity of blood'. Nevertheless, critics outside Spain racialized the Spanish as 'black' and 'Moors', allying the country with Africa and the Orient to characterize it as inherently 'savage, cruel, or tyrannical'.[42] Gautier inherits this discourse, but expands it in ways directly inspired by Ribera's paintings, which are seen as manifestations of the artist's immutable, violent identity.

For the poet, the painter is equally as dark a subject as his paintings ('le noir Valencian'), thus recalling contemporary ideas about national identity and the metaphorical connection between art and blood.[43] Towards the end of the longer poem, Gautier portrays Ribera as wanting to change his subject matter but being unable to do so: 'Un jour, las de l'horrible et des noires couleurs, / Tu voulus peindre aussi des corps blancs comme neige' (One day, weary of the horrible and the dark colours, / You also wanted to paint snow-white bodies); 'Mais tu ne sus trouver que du rouge de sang' (But you only knew how to find red blood). At the same time, the poet probes the source of the painter's dark depictions: 'D'où te vient, Ribeira, cet instinct meurtrier?' (Where does this murderous instinct come from, Ribeira?); 'Qu'avais-tu donc perdu pour être si chagrin?' (So what did you lose to become so sad?). To some extent, these are rhetorical questions since Gautier has already introduced Ribera as 'dark' by origin and unchangeable by Baptism.

42 Barbara Fuchs, "The Spanish Race" in *Rereading the Black Legend: The Discourses of Religious and Racial Difference in the Renaissance Empires*, ed. Margaret R. Greer, Walter D. Mignolo, and Maureen Quilligan (Chicago: University of Chicago Press, 2008), 95.

43 Henry Kamen, "The Myth of the Historic Nation" and "The Myth of a Christian Spain" in *Imagining Spain: Historical Myth and National Identity* (New Haven and London: Yale University Press, 2008), 1–37, 74–95.

In his longer poem on Ribera, the cries of the artist's most tortured subjects reverberate from the first to last tercet, as Gautier declares Ribera forever in search of such themes: 'Comme un autre le beau, tu cherches ce qui choque : / Les martyrs, les bourreaux, les *gitanos*, les gueux, / Étalant un ulcère à côté d'une loque' (As another seeks the beautiful, you look for what shocks: / Martyrs, executioners, *gitanos*, vagabonds, / Displaying an ulcer next to a tattered rag). Gautier invokes Bartholomew and Cato, represented in paintings on view at the Galerie Espagnole. Bartholomew is not mentioned by name, but identifiable by reference to a flayed martyr whose skin Ribera turns over 'Pour nous en faire voir l'envers ensanglanté!' (To show us the bloody underside!), a precise rendering of the executioner's action in Ribera's above-mentioned *Martyrdom of Saint Bartholomew* (fig. 3).[44] The painting of Cato is no longer attributed to Ribera, but again, Gautier perceptively renders in verse the visual rhyme between the senator's gaping wound and his screaming mouth.[45] As one who animates tortured subjects with the stroke of his brush, it appears that Ribera, in Gautier's eyes, is not simply a painter but a torturer himself: stirred by jealousy, with a 'murderous instinct', and a 'demon soul'.[46]

Nevertheless, Gautier's poems should not be read as a mere critique of Ribera's paintings. Rather than contempt, he reveals compassion for the artist – 'Les plus grands cœurs, hélas ! ont les plus grandes peines' (The greatest hearts, alas, endure the greatest suffering) – and even admiration for his quest for truth: 'Le vrai, toujours le vrai, c'est ta seule devise !' (Truth, always truth, that's your sole motto!). Furthermore, Gautier highlights the 'strange beauty' of Ribera's works and suggests that he could surpass the ancients in his ability to represent pain: 'Et tu sais revêtir d'une étrange beauté / Ces trois monstres abjects, effroi de l'art antique, / La Douleur, la Misère et la Caducité' (And you

44 Gautier was not alone in his assessment of Ribera. The French painter Jean-François Millet (1814–1875) vividly describes Ribera's painting of the *Martyrdom of Saint Bartholomew*, which he encountered at the Galerie Espagnole: 'Un bourreau à tête ignoble, et avec ce sang-froid qui n'annonce que de la cruauté, décolle la peau flétrie du vieillard en tenant le morceau d'une main et de l'autre frappant avec le poing, comme font les bouchers. On croirait entendre le craquement de la peau se détachant d'avec la chair.' 'An ignoble-looking executioner, with that cold-bloodedness which is the inevitable sign of cruelty, cuts off the old man's withered skin, holding a piece of it in one hand and with the other striking with his fist as butchers do. One can almost hear the crackling of the skin as it parts from the flesh'. Deborah L. Roldán, "Chronology" in Tinterow and Lacambre, *Manet/Velázquez*, 379.

45 Three versions of this painting are extant, and the one formerly in the Galerie Espagnole is now in the Museu Nacional d'Art de Catalunya, Barcelona. See Sílvia Blaya and Joan Yeguas, "Un *Suicidio de Catón* de Luca Giordano en el Museu Nacional d'Art de Catalunya," *Napoli nobilissima* 78 (May–August 2020): 34–44.

46 On biographical myth making, see Ernst Kris and Otto Kurz, *Legend, Myth, and Magic in the Image of the Artist: A Historical Experiment* (New Haven and London: Yale University Press, 1979), 91–132.

know how to dress with a strange beauty / Those three abject monsters, terror of ancient art, / Pain, Misery, and Caducity).

In his *Histoire du romantisme*, Gautier reminisces on the sisterhood of painting and poetry during the early nineteenth century.[47] This union of the two liberal arts, a pairing firmly grounded in the *ut pictura poesis* tradition established by Horace, does not, however, imply an equality between text and image, but rather a rivalry. The ekphrastic potential of poetry competes with the visual art of painting: the Greek philosopher Simonides declares that painting is *muta poesis* (mute poetry) while poetry is *pictura loquens* (spoken painting). Similarly, Ribera's painterly language renders Tityus's scream all but audible for viewers, while Gautier's poetic response invokes pain through resounding violent images.[48] Here, we may recall Horace's celebrated passage in his *Art of Poetry* (c. 19 BC):

> It is not enough for poetry to be beautiful; it must also be pleasing and lead the hearer's mind wherever it will. The human face smiles in sympathy with smilers and comes to the help of those that weep. If you want me to cry, mourn first yourself; *then* your misfortunes will hurt me.[49]

This passage not only suggests that to elicit a 'real' response of anguish in the reader or spectator, a fictive, yet faithful portrayal of suffering must first be constructed, but also that to arrive at such a depiction, the creator must first experience actual physical or emotional pain. Indeed, Gautier makes this observation about Ribera in his longer poem, describing him as a great suffering heart and asking: 'Qu'avais-tu donc perdu pour être si chagrin ?' (So what did you lose to become so sad?). This striking tension between fiction and reality is one which certainly resonates with the romantic and realist movements in nineteenth-century France, both literary and artistic schools in which Gautier was inextricably connected.[50]

When considering in the round Ribera's reception during the nineteenth century, it is essential to place Gautier's readings of the artist within a broader

---

47 Théophile Gautier, *Histoire du romantisme,* suivie de *Notices romantiques* et d'une *Étude sur la poésie française 1830–1868 avec un index alphabétique* (Paris: G. Charpentier et Cie, 1874), 204. For classic studies on the sister arts and the role of expression, see Rensselaer W. Lee, *Ut Pictura Poesis: The Humanistic Theory of Painting* (New York and London: W. W. Norton & Company, 1967) and Jennifer Montagu, *The Expression of the Passions: The Origin and Influence of Charles Le Brun's* Conférence sur l'expression générale et particulière (New Haven and London: Yale University Press, 1994).

48 Anthony Blunt, *Artistic Theory in Italy, 1450–1600* (Oxford and New York: Oxford University Press, 1962), 53.

49 Horace, *The Art of Poetry* in *Classical Literary Criticism*, ed. D. A. Russell and Michael Winterbottom (Oxford and New York: Oxford University Press, 1989), 100.

50 For a classic study on the evolution between romanticism and realism in nineteenth-century French painting, see Léon Rosenthal, *Du romantisme au réalisme: essai sur l'évolution de la peinture en France de 1830 à 1848* (Paris: Librairie Renouard, 1914).

context of reception history. Indeed, knowledge of Ribera in both France and Britain was largely shaped by French military campaigns and political initiatives.[51] Ribera scholars tend to gloss over the artist's revival during this period by considering his reception as embodied in, and distorted by, the lines of Byron and Gautier. To further an understanding of the artist's works and the variety of responses that they have provoked, it is necessary to provide a more nuanced, critical reading of the lens through which Ribera has been viewed by subsequent generations. In this essay, I have suggested that Gautier calls attention to the problematic relationship between the act of inflicting torture and the art of representing pain, a duality which is central to Ribera's oeuvre. To invoke Meyer Howard Abrams's terms, Gautier seems not to be holding a 'mirror' reflecting Ribera's painting, but rather a 'lamp' illuminating his artistic practice.[52]

Appendix

RIBEIRA

There are hearts filled with the sad love of the ugly.
You were one of those, painter of the coarse brush
Who Naples saluted with the name of Spagnoletto.

Nothing could soften your ferocious harshness,
And the splendid azure of the Italian sky
Has left no reflection in your cruel painting.

In your work, we always see the black Valencian,
Reckless peasant, shady beggar,
Moor that baptism hardly made a Christian.

As another seeks the beautiful, you look for what shocks:
Martyrs, executioners, *gitanos*, vagabonds,
Displaying an ulcer next to a tattered rag;

Old men with a rocking head and a rough yellow hide,
Pouring over some Bible a flood of grey beard;
That's what suits your fiery brush.

You disdain nothing that is despised;
No rag, Ribeira, is rejected by you:
Truth, always truth, that's your sole motto!

51 Alisa Luxenberg, *The Galerie Espagnole and the Museo Nacional 1835–1853: Saving Spanish Art, or the Politics of Patrimony* (Aldershot: Ashgate Publishing, 2008), 13–54.
52 Meyer Howard Abrams, *The Mirror and the Lamp: Romantic Theory and the Critical Tradition* (New York: W. W. Norton & Company, 1958).

And you know how to dress with a strange beauty
Those three abject monsters, terror of ancient art,
Pain, Misery, and Caducity.

For you, neither Apollo, nor chaste Venus;
You allow not one of these lovely white dreams
Carved from Parian or Pentelic marble.

You need dark and violent subjects
Where the angel of sorrows empties his black chalices,
Where the axe is blunted by the dripping execution block.

You seem intoxicated by the wine of torture,
Like a Roman Caesar insulted in his crimson robe,
Or like an executioner after twenty sacrifices.

With what fury and what voluptuousness
You turn over the skin of the martyr that is flayed,
To show us the bloody underside!

How you hold the flame to the feet of the condemned!
How you make the opening in Cato's side scream,
Horrible wound, yawning like an entrance!

Where does this murderous instinct come from, Ribeira?
What tooth bit you, who gives you rage,
To so twist the human species and crush it?

So what has the world done to you, and, in all this carnage,
What secret enemy do you pursue with your blows?
So what offence provoked such bloodshed?

This martyr is the body of a fallen rival;
And it's not always the heart of Prometheus
That the tawny eagle probes with its pointed beak.

What ambition cast down from heaven,
What hope dragged by unbridled steeds,
Stirred your demon soul?

So what did you lose to become so sad?
What twisted loves formed your hatreds,
And who made you jealous, you, sovereign painter?

The greatest hearts, alas, endure the greatest suffering;
In the deep cut there are more pains;
Heaven thus seeks revenge on human glories.

One day, weary of the horrible and the dark colours,
You also wanted to paint snow-white bodies,
Smiling angels, birds, and flowers,

Nymphs in the woods besieged by the satyr,
Cupids sleeping on a quivering breast,
And all those fresh motifs dear to the mellow Correggio;

But you only knew how to find red blood,
And when the angel of God descends from heaven,
To lay the halo on the forehead of your saints,

Averting his eyes, he puts it down and flies away!

Hans Erik Havsteen
(University of Copenhagen)

Whose Triumph? The Reception History of Bertel Thorvaldsen's Frieze *Alexander the Great's Entry into Babylon* (1812)

Abstract
The neoclassical sculptor Bertel Thorvaldsen's (1770–1844) art has rarely been examined in a political context although his art was commissioned by liberals and conservatives alike. This article seeks to rectify this deficiency by examining one of Thorvaldsen's most famous works, the *Alexander Frieze,* and the history of its reception in a political context. The article explores how the frieze, which was commissioned by Napoleon I, reflects the relationship between art and power in the period and how this relationship evolved during Thorvaldsen's lifetime.
The article demonstrates that Thorvaldsen had a conflicted relationship with the concept of monarchy and that contemporaries claimed that Thorvaldsen expressed subtle criticism of Napoleon in the frieze. The reception history of the frieze until 1850 will illustrate how Thorvaldsen gained artistic independence while his art was also appropriated to satisfy the ideological needs of various political factions.

Keywords
Alexander the Great, Napoleon I, neoclassicism, political art, romanticism

Introduction

The Danish neoclassical sculptor Bertel Thorvaldsen's (1770–1844) plaster frieze *Alexander the Great's Entry into Babylon* secured its creator fame throughout Europe. The frieze was commissioned by the French court to decorate the Quirinal Palace in Rome in honour of Emperor Napoleon I's – eventually cancelled – visit to the 'Eternal City' in 1812, where it is still on display. The artwork is highly revealing of how Thorvaldsen acted politically and of the evolving relationship between power and art in the period in general.

In the decades following the French Revolution, social change swept over Europe, and the history of the *Alexander Frieze* is an illustrative example of this. Bertel Thorvaldsen had an ambiguous relationship with Napoleon, and the primary source material indicates that the frieze could be interpreted as more than a mere tribute to the French emperor. Numerous copies were produced, and the frieze became part of the political communication in Europe in the subsequent decades. By creating the frieze, Thorvaldsen found himself in the middle of the most intense political conflict of his time, between absolute and constitutional monarchy, between Germanic and Latin culture, and between the old world and emerging modern society.

However, the literature on the *Alexander Frieze* in particular, and on Thorvaldsen's art in a political context in general, is rather limited. Neither the political circumstances concerning the commissioning, execution, and display of the frieze, nor the frieze's reception history have scarcely been examined in depth. In this article, it is my intention to explore how Bertel Thorvaldsen can be perceived as a political artist through his work on the *Alexander Frieze,* as well as examining the artwork's contemporary reception history, which offers a unique insight into the political, social, and cultural change Europe underwent during those crucial years after the French Revolution.

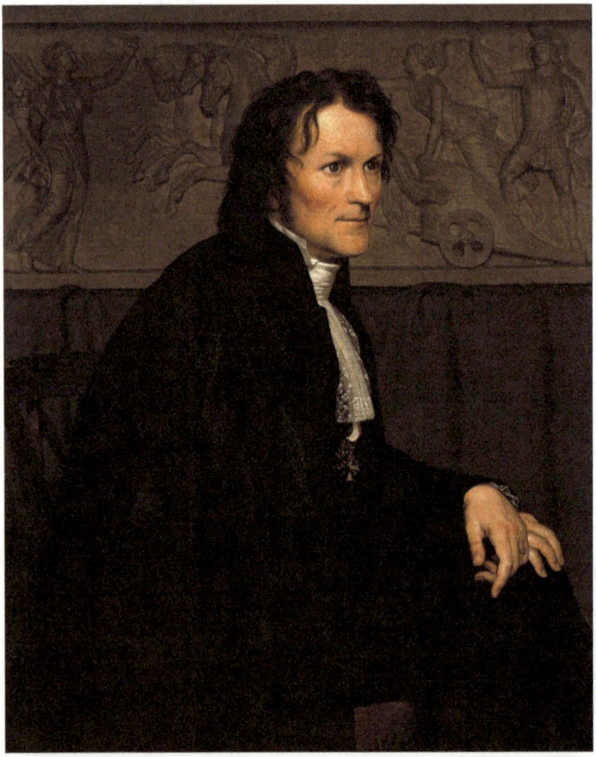

Figure 1. C.W. Eckersberg, *Portrait of Bertel Thorvaldsen* (with the Alexander Frieze in the background), 1814, oil on canvas, Academy of Fine Arts, Copenhagen.

Historiography of the *Alexander Frieze*

There has, from the latter part of the 19th century and until at least the middle of the 20th century, been a strong tendency among scholars to discard neo-classicism as a dull and tedious reproduction of antiquity. The judgement of Bertel Thorvaldsen and his art has come to suffer from this distorted view, which is neatly summed up in the following quotation by the American art historian Robert Rosenblum (1927–2006):

> Contemporary taste has been harsh in its judgement of Neoclassicism. Prizing originality, we are critical of a style which was willing to pay homage, at times even servile homage, to a past considered greater than the present. ... Even such great masters as David and Canova are often discussed in a manner which implies that their veneration of antiquity was an unfortunate, if inevitable handicap dictated by the taste of their generation; and lesser figures like West and Thorvaldsen are not infrequently dismissed by art historians with little more than a tolerant smile.[1]

But to describe the work of David, Canova, or Thorvaldsen as a 'servile homage' is a biased reading of their work. For instance, the research project 'The Thorvaldsen Museum Archives', which ran from 2006–2021, has taken important steps to uncover and examine primary sources such as letters, diary excerpts, poems, and newspaper articles which point in the direction of forgotten and/or ignored political dimensions in Thorvaldsen's art. It has here been established, that Thorvaldsen subscribed to, among other things, the egalitarian ideals of the French Revolution and was keen to see restrictions imposed on the power of the absolutist monarchies of Europe. His preoccupation with these ideas can be detected in several of his works and monuments.[2]

Another important factor in the negligence of neoclassicism as a political art form has probably been the conflicted view in the 19th and 20th centuries of romanticism's relationship with politics, especially that of German romanticism.[3] Except in Arnold Hauser's work *The Social History of Art* (1951), neoclassicism has also tended to evade the interest of social art history. Hauser's work has been criticised, although Peter Burke has recently argued for the relevance and revival

1 Robert Rosenblum: "Review of *Klassizismus und Utopia; Interpretationen zu Werken von David, Canova, Carstens, Thorvaldsen, Koch*" by Rudolf Zeitler. *The Art Bulletin*, Vol. 37, No. 1, (March 1955): 70–4. https://doi.org/10.2307/3047599.

2 Nanna Kronberg Frederiksen, "Christian 8.'s Loan from Thorvaldsen", arkivet.thorvaldsens-museum. dk, 2014; Ernst Jonas Bencard, "Thorvaldsen's Continuance in Rome 1803–4", arkivet.thorvaldsensmuseum.dk, 2009; Hans Erik Havsteen, "An Ambiguous Monument", arkivet.thorvaldsensmuseum.dk, 2017.

3 Frederick C. Beiser, *Enlightenment, Revolution, and Romanticism – The Genesis of Modern German Political Thought, 1790–1800*, (Cambridge: Harvard University Press, 1992), 85, 222–7 and Suzanne L. Marchand, *Down from Olympus – Archaeology and Philhellenism in Germany 1750–1970*, (New Jersey: Princeton University Press, 1996), 3–7.

of social art history.[4] As exemplified in Tim Blanning's book *The Culture of Power and The Power of Culture* and to a lesser degree *The Romantic Revolution*, the social history of art is difficult, if not impossible, to separate from politics. This underlines the need to re-examine neoclassicism in its social context to help illuminate its political influence on historical developments in the early 19th century.

Thorvaldsen was considered a member of the very elite of German artists by his peers, an artistic elite whose political affiliations have been the subject of much debate in the 20th century. The 'unpolitical' nature of the German *Bildungsbürgertum* (educated bourgeoisie) was scrutinized following the debacle of the Second World War. Schiller's letters on aesthetics for instance, have been branded his 'flight from politics' following the war.[5] Another important figure (and a close friend of Thorvaldsen), Wilhelm von Humboldt has also been described as unpolitical and the German romantic preoccupation with education (Bildung) has since been interpreted as a lack of political interest. This however has been refuted by among others Frederick C. Beiser who stresses the political nature of the German romantic *Bildungsideal,* which strove to improve society and cultivate its citizens through proper education, emphasising above all the political importance of arts and aesthetics in Romanticism.[6]

Beiser asserts that the Romantics can be perceived as much more than members of a literary movement only. They were in his view important political thinkers, inspired by among others Herder, who with their emphasis on (German) vernacular traditions stood in opposition to the (French) universal and cosmopolitan 'shallowness' of the Enlightenment. The romantic preoccupation with the spirit of the German people had comprehensive political consequences since it seriously challenged the authoritarian rule of the numerous German princes around 1800 as well as later resisting the foreign intervention of Napoleon's France.

The exhibition 'I nederlagets skygge. Guldalderens glemte kunstnere' (In the Shadow of Defeat. The Forgotten Artists of the Danish Golden Age) from 2023 at the Danish Museum Kunstmuseet Brundlund Slot, curated by Sine Krogh and Sally Schlosser Schmidt, tackles the same problem from a Danish point of view. Danish romantic art is understood to have been deeply political and attached to various identities and nationalities within the Danish conglomerate state. The salient issue in this context was the struggle for various forms of government, in

4 Peter Burke, "The Social Histories of Art" in *The Art Market in Rome in the Eighteenth Century: A Study in the Social History of Art*, ed. Paulo Coen (Leiden: Brill, 2018), 28. https://doi.org/10.1163/9789004388154_003.
5 Beiser, *Enlightenment,* 85.
6 Beiser, *Enlightenment,* 84–140.

which the art was used as a political means of communication by different political milieus.

As such, various factors have resulted in negligence or misreading of important source material concerning Thorvaldsen's life and work. The social and political impact of neoclassical art was thus not properly recognised for a long time, which has also influenced the judgement of Thorvaldsen and his art. This omission has led to several important characteristics being missed. It was, in the words of the antiquarian Johann Joachim Winckelmann, the job of the neoclassical artist to imitate - not copy - antiquity.[7]

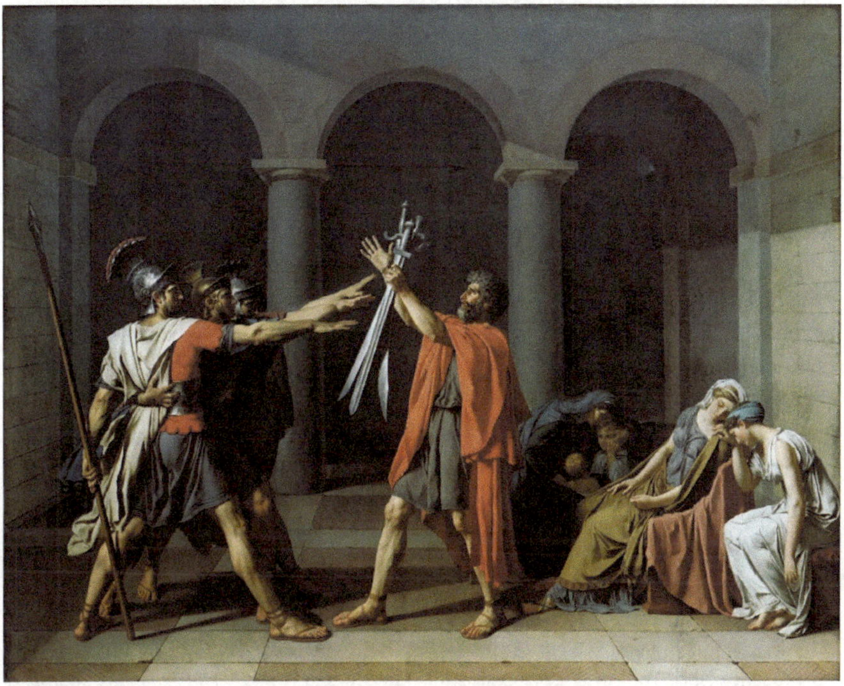

Figure 2. Jacques-Louis David, *The Oath of the Horatii*, 1784, oil on canvas, Musée de Louvre, Paris.

Discarding neoclassical artists' preoccupation with antiquity as 'unfortunate' thus ignores important, artistic messages. David, whose painting *The Oath of the Horatii* from 1784 (fig. 2) was instrumental in defining the neoclassical style, was hardly a 'servile homage' to the past. Rather it was an active political stance on

7 James L. Larson, "Winckelmann's Essay on Imitation," Eighteenth-Century Studies, Vol. 9, No. 3 (Spring, 1976): 390–405. https://doi.org/10.2307/2737517.

the present as it conveyed revolutionary messages, as argued by, among others, Thomas Crow and Kenneth Clark.[8]

Ambiguous messages and/or embedded criticism has been an important component of panegyric (which is also adaptable to visual art) ever since antiquity, which both patrons and audiences exploited.[9] It is therefore crucial to note the differences in political mentalities between now and then. The political systems in Europe in the 19th century mostly prohibited overt political statements, at least if they worked against the ideology of the regime. Early 19th century art, which contains messages with subtle criticism of a ruling regime, is thus easy to overlook from a modern perspective. Artists' political agency can be complicated to discern in an authoritarian society as outspoken critique of a ruling regime would often have been either censored or outright punished.

The fact that Thorvaldsen belonged mostly to a German culture and context, might also have resulted in him being overlooked in the French dominated scholarship of neoclassicism.[10] The Danish nationalistic emphasis on Thorvaldsen's art has tended to blur the understanding of and the European context in which his art came into being. Thorvaldsen's first biographer, the Danish civil servant Just Mathias Thiele (1795–1874), effectively shaped later generations' nationalistic and apolitical view of Thorvaldsen.[11] Many scholars have since emphasised that it was Thorvaldsen's 'unpolitical' attitude, which secured him commissions from all over Europe, although a few scholars have indeed recognised political aspects in Thorvaldsen's art.[12]

But most of the (limited) scholarly literature on the frieze either abstains from assessing whether political motifs can be found in the *Alexander Frieze* either due to neglect or to perceived uncertainties and/or concludes that Thorvaldsen held no political opinions.[13] Furthermore, it is a general rule that the scholarly

8 Kenneth Clark, *The Romantic Rebellion – Romantic versus Classic Art*, (London: Sotheby Parke Bernet Publications Ltd., 1973) p. 21.

9 Frederick Ahl: "The Art of Safe Criticism in Greece and Rome", *The American Journal of Philology*, Vol. 105, No. 2 (Spring, 1984), 174–208. https://doi.org/10.2307/294874.

10 Christopher Johns, *Antonio Canova and the Politics of Patronage in Revolutionary and Napoleonic Europe*, (London: University of California Press, 1998), 4; David d'Angers, "Lettre sur Thorwaldsen", 19.4.1844, *Småtryk 1856* (The Thorvaldsen Museum Archives, Copenhagen.)

11 Just Mathias Thiele, 1832: *Den danske Billedhugger Bertel Thorvaldsen og hans Værker, Anden Deel, tekst- og planchebind*, (Copenhagen, 1832) and Just Mathias Thiele, *II: Thorvaldsen i Rom. 1805–1819*, (Copenhagen, 1852).

12 Jürgen Wittstock, *Geschichte der Deutschen und Skandinavischen Thorwaldsen-Rezeption bis zur Jahresmitte 1819*, (Hamburg, 1975): 14.

13 Bjarne Jørnæs, "Thorvaldsen's Triumph of Alexander", (Analecta Romana Instituti Danici, 1989), p. 40, https://doi.org/10.1163/9789004359932_023, Fredrik Thomasson, "Art, Nationalism and Politics during Occupation and Restoration Rome: "Che razza infame, quella dei leccaculi!"" in ed. Stefano FogelbergRota & Sabrina Norlander Eliasson, *The City of the Soul:*

literature lacks a thorough analysis of the frieze's political impact on European society in the decades that followed its execution in 1812 and until the revolutions of 1848.

The availability of a more comprehensive body of source material today enables a thorough and bolder re-examination of the frieze and the history surrounding it. The sources examined are predominantly found among The Thorvaldsen Museum Archives' digital collection of more than 10,000 documents, all easily accessible regardless of their physical location across Europe. This variety of text genres (letters, diary entries, contracts, newspaper articles, and poems) will be augmented by a few other printed sources (mostly letters) located outside this archive.

Political Neoclassicism

The societal role of the artist was evolving dramatically in the decades around 1800, just as all parts of Western societies were.[14] This development occurred alongside the emergence of a 'public sphere' across Western Europe in particular and was widely felt in the artistic sphere.[15] A new generation of highly individualistic artists came not only to represent the new revolutionary world but were also expected to help shape and define it.[16] This artistic movement had been in the making since at least the 1770s, but the events in France helped to radicalise it in many places in Europe. The German poet and philosopher Friedrich Schiller (1759–1805) even went so far as to recognise the artist as an important political force, equal to both princes, priests, and philosophers.[17]

Not only did the preferred artistic style shift from rococo to neoclassicism, but the conception of the artist changed too. A new world view began to take hold in the 1790s, especially in Britain and Germany, partly inspired by and partly provoked by the events in France. The romantic idea of the artist as a profound,

---

The Literary Making of Rome, (Rome, 2015),172–5, Tabea Schindler, *Bertel Thorvaldsen – Celebrity: Visualisierungen eines Künstlerkults im frühen 19. Jahrhundert,* (Berlin: de Gruyter, 2021), 77–8. O.P. Calmeyer, "Die Orientalen auf Thorvaldsens Alexanderfries", in *Achaemenid history* 5. Ed. H. Sancisi-Weerdenburg & J.W. Drijvers, (Leiden: Nederlands Inst. voor het Nabije Oosten, 1990), 113.

14 Tim Blanning, *The Power of Culture and The Culture of Power*, (Oxford: Oxford University Press, 2002), 91.

15 Blanning, *The Power of Culture* 5–15 & 181–2.

16 See Thomas Crow, *Emulation: Making Artists for Revolutionary France*, (London: Yale University Press, 1995) for a thorough discussion of this topic.

17 Friedrich Schiller, *On the Aesthetic Education of Man in a Series of Letters – English and German Facing*, eds. Elizabeth Wilkinson & L.A. Willoughby (Oxford: Oxford University Press, 1967), 57–61.

revolutionary force was born. It was into this context Thorvaldsen entered when he arrived in Rome in 1797. It might seem confusing to label Thorvaldsen both a romantic and neoclassical artist, since the two categories are often described as contrasts to one another.[18] But it must be stressed that whereas neoclassicism is a distinct artistic style, the term romanticism does not describe a recognisable artistic style in the visual arts.[19]

Thorvaldsen had been born into poverty in the Danish-Norwegian capital of Copenhagen in 1770 but was admitted to the Academy of Fine Arts in Copenhagen when he was still a boy. Here, his talent was quickly recognised and, in 1796, he gained a scholarship and went to Rome. The stipend was to last for around three years with the option of prolonging it, but ultimately Thorvaldsen ended up staying in Rome for more than forty years, rather than returning to the service of the Danish king. His unwillingness to return to the provincial Danish capital can be interpreted in a political light and might have been inspired by the German-Danish painter Asmus Jacob Carstens' (1754–1798) refusal to return to the service of the Prussian king.[20] Carstens was one of Thorvaldsen's closest acquaintances during his first year in Rome.

Ever since Thorvaldsen's own decision to stay in Rome in 1803–4, the idea of personal and artistic autonomy therefore appeared to have been of great importance to Thorvaldsen as well.[21] But Thorvaldsen was not as candid as Carstens, and few (if any) direct political views are expressed in his existing correspondence. Thorvaldsen's apparent lack of academic skill as well as the absence of clear political views have clouded the scholarly view of Thorvaldsen for a long time. Although political utterances are missing from Thorvaldsen's own hand, documents from Thorvaldsen's social circle confirm in abundance that he held political views as well as political and personal prejudices.

The actress Johanne Luise Heiberg (1812–90) describes Thorvaldsen as taciturn but with a dry sense of humour. She notes that his repeated refusals of dinner invitations from the Danish king Christian VIII (1786–1848, reigned from 1839) had nothing to do with political naivety and disregard of social conventions as claimed by some observers but was rather a clear sign of Thorvaldsen's egalitarian dispositions.[22] To refuse an invitation from such a prestigious host was

---

18 For a further discussion of Thorvaldsen as either a neoclassical or romantic artist please see the catalogue *Schönheit und Revolution: Klassizismus 1770–1820*,ed. M. Bückling and E. Mongi-Vollmer (Munich: Städtische Galerie im Städelschen Kunstinstitut Frankfurt am Main, 2013).

19 Hugh Honour, *Romanticism*, 15.

20 Tim Blanning, *The Romantic Revolution – A History, (New York: Weidenfeld & Nicolson, 2010)*, 20.

21 Ernst Jonas Bencard, "Thorvaldsen's Continuance in Rome 1803–04".

22 Johanne Luise Heiberg, *Et Liv gjenoplevet i Erindringen af Johanne Luise Heiberg vol. 2*, (København, 1944 [1891–92]), 29–33.

generally unheard of at the time. In general, Thorvaldsen seemed to have had an ambiguous relationship with the Danish monarchy and in particular Christian VIII.[23]

One further anecdote illustrates Thorvaldsen's preoccupation with egalitarian values. During his way back to Copenhagen after a trip to Rome in 1842, when his stardom had been cemented, Thorvaldsen was celebrated in every city he passed through. On one such celebratory occasion in Altona, after dinner, Thorvaldsen shook the hand of every person present: Not only the gentlemen, but the women and children too, and most important of all: the servants in the kitchen.[24] This gesture caused sensation in the hierarchial society of the day. He was labelled *Paradigmata der Menschheit,* and the story was widely disseminated thereafter.[25]

An interesting letter to Thorvaldsen, which concerns his relationship to the concepts of monarchy and liberty, is probably written in the summer of 1842 by Marie Lehmann (1821–49) who was married to the prominent Danish liberal politician Orla Lehmann (1810–70). The Thorvaldsen Museum was then under construction, and Marie claims that her mother risked causing political trouble when she hoisted the French tricolour over the unfinished museum. Marie, however, thought this political statement to be fitting since it was obvious to her that Thorvaldsen's art represented the concept of freedom, and that the museum as such should be free of any royal or state interference.[26]

So, although Thorvaldsen hardly made any direct political statements in writing, his actions, actions made on his behalf, comments on his behaviour and opinions made by those around him, indicate a political stance which at the very least can be said to be critical towards the existing power structures in society, seriously challenging the claim that Thorvaldsen was an unpolitical artist. On the contrary Thorvaldsen's own life, work and way of behaving came to be seen as the embodiment and synthesis of the revolutionary ideal by many contemporaries.[27]

23 Heiberg, *Et Liv gjenoplevet*, 29–33;Kronberg Frederiksen., "Christian 8.s Loan".

24 Giuseppe Mugnoz, "Letter to Bertel Thorvaldsen", Earliest 14th of August, latest 1st of December 1831. m30 II, nr. 78a, The Thorvaldsen Museum Archives, Copenhagen. Salomon Ludwig Steinheim, 'Ein Zusammentreffen mit Thorvaldsen auf der Lüneburger Heide', in: *Telegraph für Deutschland* November 1842, Nr. 188, 749–752 & Christine Stampe, *Baronesse Stampes Erindringer om Thorvaldsen*, ed. Rigmor Stampe, (København 1912), 179–180.

25 Johanna Steinheim, "Letter to Raphael Hanno", 29th of October 1842. m30 II, nr. 78, The Thorvaldsen Museum Archives: Copenhagen.

26 Marie Lehmann: "Letter to Bertel Thorvaldsen", Summer of 1842, m24 1842, nr. 63, The Thorvaldsen Museum Archives, Copenhagen.

27 Mugnoz, "Letter to Bertel Thorvaldsen".

The Commissioning of the Frieze

The historical circumstances behind the commissioning of Thorvaldsen's *Alexander Frieze* for the Quirinal Palace were highly dramatic. The conflict between Napoleon I and Pope Pius VII, which had been brewing ever since Pius became pope in 1800, came to a head in 1809, when Napoleon abducted the ageing pope from the Quirinal Palace in Rome and put him in prison in Fontainebleau. Since the pope had unwillingly vacated the city, Napoleon now saw a chance to turn Rome into the empire's second city, culturally linking the ancient Roman empire with his modern French one.[28]

In 1811 the architect Raffaele Stern (1774–1820) embarked on a grand project of renovation so that the palace could properly accommodate the imperial family for its scheduled visit in 1812. The extensive renovation was typical for Napoleon's imperial project and similar projects had been initiated all over the French sphere of influence in Europe, where they were generally characterised by lavish budgets.[29] Thorvaldsen's frieze was 35.2 meters long and 1.17 meters tall and covered all four walls in the 'Hall of Honour'.

Napoleon's association with Alexander the Great was far from new. The comparison with Alexander had been obvious to make ever since Napoleon's political and military breakthrough in the 1790s.[30] But although Napoleon supported these propaganda comparisons, the use of Alexander did have its negative sides, too. For was Alexander a great hero or a vain tyrant? After Napoleon's second marriage to Marie Louise of Austria in 1810 the allegorical comparisons with Alexander ceased to be commissioned.[31] In the alliance with his former enemy Austria, Napoleon wished to send less bellicose signals in his propaganda. Thorvaldsen's *Alexander Frieze* constitutes an important exception to this rule.

It was also the first time Thorvaldsen depicted the ancient Macedonian hero, and he would only return to him once after the *Alexander Frieze,* namely in 1831, when Thorvaldsen executed a relief depicting Alexander burning down the Persian ceremonial capital of Persepolis (fig. 3). This depiction of the ancient hero is in stark contrast to the peaceful Alexander in Babylon, rather focusing on

28 Michael Broers, *Napoleon - The Spirit of the Age 1805–1810*, (London: Pegasus Books, 2018), 439 & Stefano Grandesso, *Bertel Thorvaldsen (1770–1844)*, (Milan: Silvana, 2018), 103.

29 Philip Mansel, *The Eagle in Splendour - Inside the Court of Napoleon,* (London: I.B. Tauris, 2015), 67–72.

30 Broers, *Spirit of the Age,* 141–42.

31 Agnieszka Fulińska, "Alexander and Napoleon" in ed. Kenneth Royce Moore, *Brill's Companion to the Reception of Alexander the Great,* Series: Brill's Companions to Classical Reception; volume 14, (Leiden: Brill, 2018), 567. https://doi.org/10.1163/9789004359932_023.

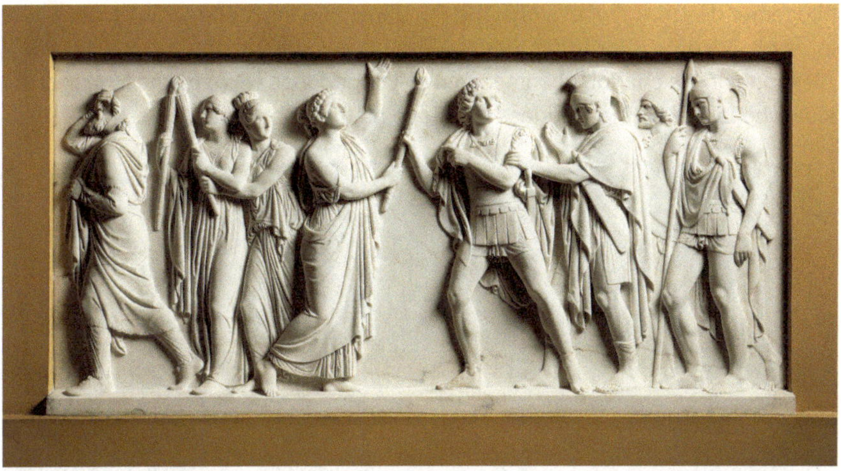

Figure 3. Bertel Thorvaldsen, *Alexander the Great Provoked by Thaïs to Set Fire to Persepolis*, 1832, marble, The Thorvaldsen Museum, Copenhagen.

the drunk prince, who in anger burns down a defenceless city. One can't help but wonder whether this later relief, commissioned by the Bavarian monarch, was a comment on both the original *Alexander Frieze* from 1812 and Napoleon's destructive occupation of Moscow the same year.

It remains unclear to which extent Thorvaldsen himself chose the iconography of Alexander in March 1812, but acceptance for the overall iconographic programme was needed from the French imperial representatives, who reported back to Napoleon in detail.[32] We can only guess as to why Napoleon accepted the motif of Alexander, but Thorvaldsen's emphasis on peaceful motifs in the frieze (which was in line with Napoleon's new propaganda programme) might have been a contributing factor. In any case, an awareness seems to have existed concerning the ambiguity of using Alexander as an allegory in art, both from the perspective of the patron, the artist, and the public.

Thorvaldsen had been inspired by the famous Parthenon frieze made for the Parthenon Temple in the city-state of Athens in the 5th century BC by the renowned sculptor Pheidias.[33] Thorvaldsen relied on the Roman historian Curtius Rufus' work *Histories of Alexander the Great* for narrative inspiration and the Swedish orientalist Johan David Åkerblad for advice on ancient Babylon. Although Thorvaldsen was inspired by the Parthenon frieze, a crucial difference separates his modern *Alexander Frieze* from the ancient Greek one. Whereas a single procession in the Parthenon frieze heads for the end of the frieze, two

32 Ibid., 568.

33 Grandesso, *Thorvaldsen*, 108–9.

altogether different processions, the Persians, and the Macedonians, are found in Thorvaldsen's *Alexander Frieze.* They converge on the central figure of Alexander in his chariot (accompanied by the goddess Nike) on the Macedonian side who is met by the Goddess of Peace on the Babylonian side.

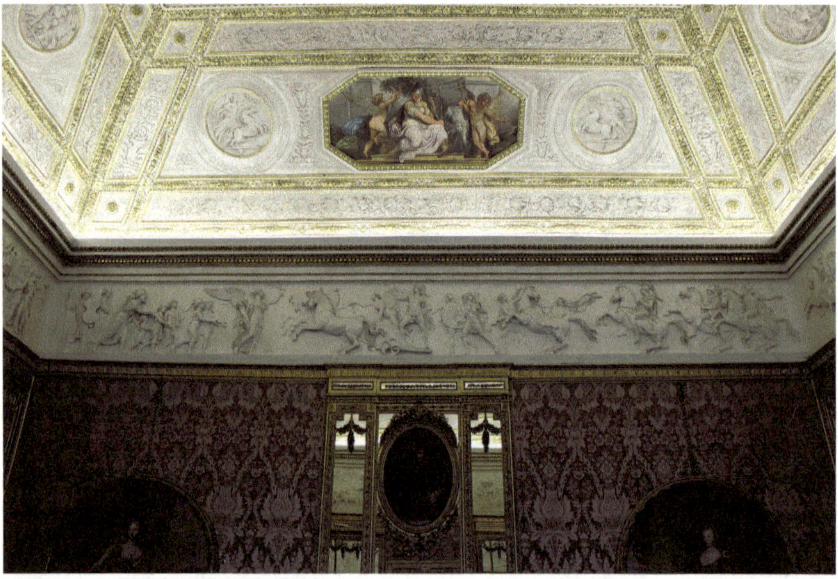

Figure 4. Bertel Thorvaldsen. *Alexander the Great's Entry into Babylon*, 1812, plaster, Palazzo Quirinale, Rome.

Alexander is followed by his soldiers, cavalry, and infantry alike, as well as his horse Bucephalus. The triumphant soldiers bring with them a captured Persian nobleman as well as an elephant carrying looted treasures. At the very end of the Macedonian procession Thorvaldsen depicted himself underneath a palm tree (possibly signifying triumph) overseeing the entry into Babylon.

The other procession is made up by the vanquished Persians, where the submissive satrap and governor of the city, Mazaeus, can be seen directly behind the Goddess of Peace in the company of his small children who are pushed towards the Macedonians. He is followed by Persian women throwing flowers in the path of Alexander and his army. An altar is prepared, and animals brought forward as a present to the victorious army along with the astrologers of Babylon, scenes of everyday life and the river god of Tigris.

In the last part of the relief, merchants are leaving Babylon with their goods, and a fisherman is fishing peacefully underneath the palm trees with his dog.

Thorvaldsen's frieze quickly stood out as the artwork everyone spoke of in Rome. In one of the leading German magazines of the day, *Morgenblatt für*

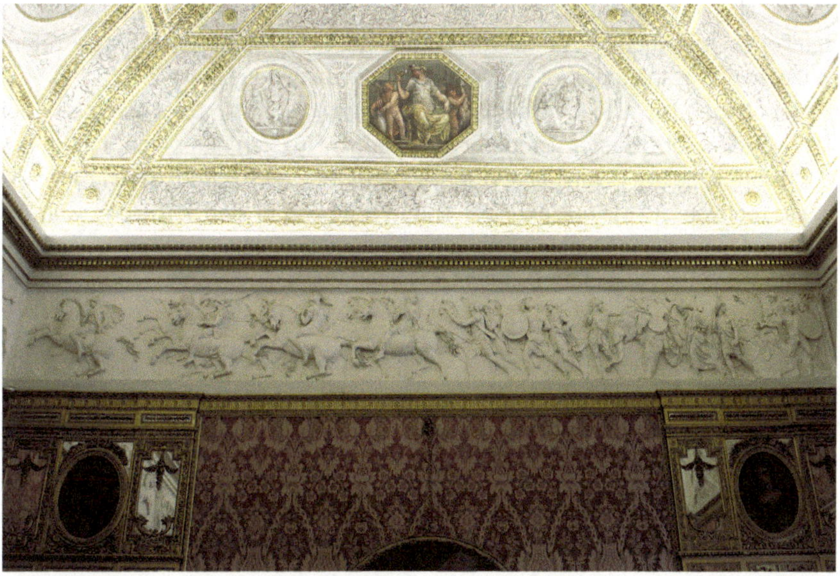

Figure 5. Bertel Thorvaldsen. Alexander the Great's Entry into Babylon, 1812, plaster, Palazzo Quirinale, Rome.

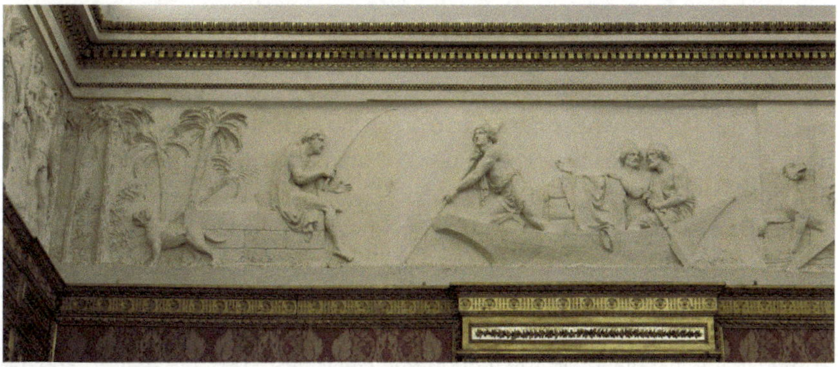

Figure 6. Bertel Thorvaldsen. Detail of *Alexander the Great's Entry into Babylon*, 1812, plaster, Palazzo Quirinale, Rome.

Gebildete Stände, the Baltic German author Carl Gotthard Grass describes the brand-new frieze in October 1812 and draws attention to the Italians who dubbed Thorvaldsen the *Patriarch of the Bas-relief* in recognition of his effort.[34] The frieze's connection to Napoleon is hardly mentioned. Instead, Grass emphasises that it is made in a 'truly Greek style' and that the Italians found the work to be

34 Carl Gotthard Grass, 'Korrespondenznachrichten', *Morgenblatt für Gebildete Stände*, nr. 254, 22.10.1812, 1015–16.

'classical', two great compliments at the time. Thorvaldsen had returned to the spirit of Greek antiquity, but with 'new motifs' as Grass points out. It was a 'return to the spirit, not the letter, of antiquity' to quote James L. Larson.[35]

Simultaneously with the installation of the artwork, the frieze's commissioner was heading for disaster. Emperor Napoleon's Russian campaign ended in a catastrophic defeat in the fall and winter of 1812, a defeat from which he would never recover. Just like Alexander ended up dying in Babylon along with his empire, Napoleon too would suffer death in Moscow, albeit metaphorically. For his army and the Russian population however, the suffering and death was quite literal.

The Pragmatic Artist

Was it hypocrisy that made Thorvaldsen sympathise with the liberal cause and egalitarian values on one hand, while on the other accepting commissions (and money) from authoritarian princes like Napoleon? It may appear contradictory that Thorvaldsen should do both, but although the sculptor may have been politically progressive, he still relied on the support of conservative monarchies in Europe, not only for income but also simply to receive permission to work.

A poignant example of this concerns Thorvaldsen's presence at the Conference of Troppau in October 1820, where the conservative powers of Austria, Prussia, and Russia convened to discuss an intervention against the democratic revolution in Naples, which had taken place in the summer of 1820. It would seem bizarre that Thorvaldsen showed up at a conference destined for crushing democratic movements.

But Thorvaldsen had, back in 1817, been commissioned to execute a monument of the Polish national hero Prince Poniatowski who had fought for Napoleon and fell in the battle of Leipzig in 1813. Poniatowski's old enemy, the Russian emperor Alexander I (who now also ruled Poland as king), had initially agreed to the installation of the monument. But it was a delicate matter, and the monument remained to be executed and installed in 1820.

Shortly before the Conference in Troppau, Thorvaldsen modelled a bust of Alexander I in Warsaw (fig. 8). A submissive letter from Thorvaldsen to Alexander notifying the emperor of the finished artwork, in which Thorvaldsen wrote:

35 Larson, "Winckelmann's Essay on Imitation," 390.

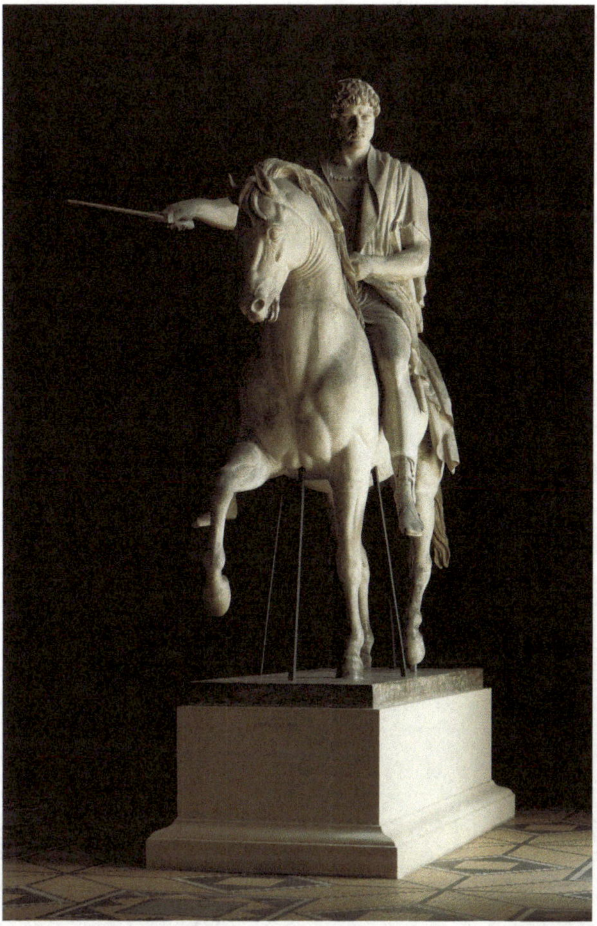

Figure 7. Bertel Thorvaldsen, *Monument to Józef Poniatowski*, 1826, plaster, The Thorvaldsen Museum, Copenhagen.

> Il sera à jamais l'époque la plus heureuse de ma vie, où il me fut donné de contempler de près le plus grand Monarque de la terre (It will forever be the happiest time of my life, when I had the chance to contemplate the greatest monarch on earth up close).[36]

This formal expression indicates that Thorvaldsen was hugely aware of the importance of accommodating the whims of powerful sovereigns. The letter was written by Thorvaldsen's friend Peter Ole Brøndsted, who was an experienced diplomat and the Danish agent at the papal court (only the signature belongs to Thorvaldsen personally), which also underlines Thorvaldsen's proximity to pro-

36 Bertel Thorvaldsen, "Letter to Tsar Alexander I", 24th of May 1822. Arkhiv Vneshnei Politiki Rossiskoi Imperii, Moscow. Unless otherwise noted, all translations are my own.

fessional Danish diplomats. They may have emphasized the importance of diplomatic etiquette in Thorvaldsen's dealings with princely clients.

The history behind a monument to Frederik VI in Skanderborg, Denmark reflects the same themes. Thorvaldsen was commissioned in 1840 by several prominent liberal Danish citizens to execute a monument commemorating the late King Frederik VI. When examining the primary sources at hand, it is evident that the apparent tribute to Frederik VI was only part of the message the patrons wished to communicate.

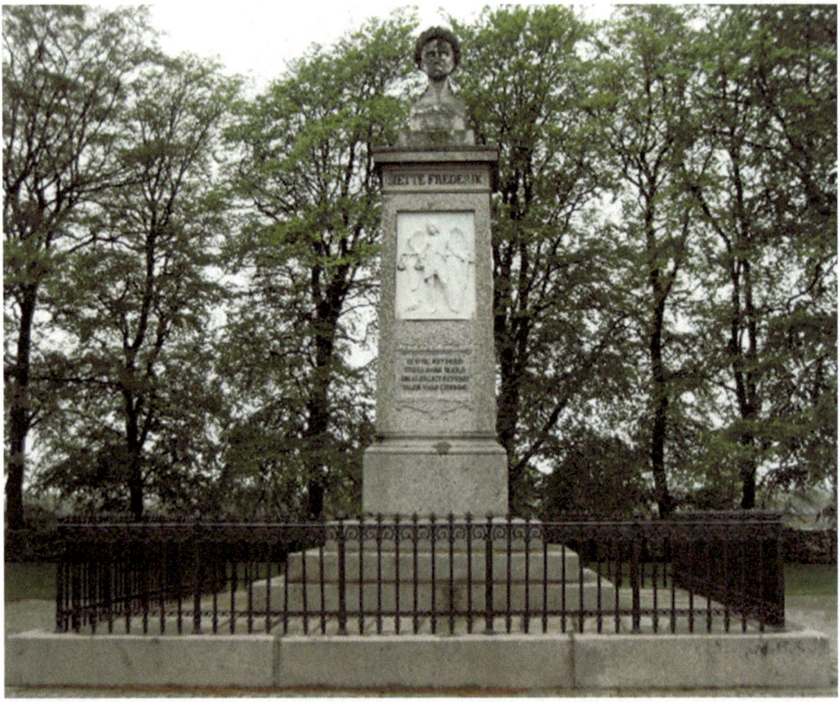

Figure 8. Bertel Thorvaldsen, Monument to Frederik VI, 1845, marble, Skanderborg Slotsbanke, Denmark.

Applauding the late conservative king for his (few) progressive reforms, but emphasising that the monument was a *memorial,* rather than a monument of *liberty* (which wouldn't be erected until the king had accepted a free constitution) effectively put a lot of pressure on the new king Christian VIII and encouraged him to speed up the process concerning a free constitution.[37] But such claims could not be directly expressed in an absolute monarchy, which meant that the de-

37 Hans Erik Havsteen, 'An Ambiguous Monument', arkivet.thorvaldsensmuseum.dk, 2017.

mands had to be somewhat disguised. Art was the perfect medium in which to present these veiled requests.

Thorvaldsen had to work within the confines of monarchy and respect the political situation of the time even though he might have held views which supported freedom and egalitarian values. But he had to be a diplomat besides his artistic profession if he was to succeed (and thus enlisted and employed help from his social circle).

Artist vs. Emperor

Not even a year after Thorvaldsen's arrival in the Pope's city, the French had occupied much of Italy and would continue to exert heavy influence right up until Napoleon's own downfall in the years 1812–14. Apart from the uneasy peace of Amiens in 1802–1803, Europe was tormented by continuous warfare until 1815, and it would have been impossible for Thorvaldsen to ignore this in Rome.

Resistance, as well as collaboration, to French rule characterised Rome in the years under French dominance.[38] The French looting of the city's treasures of art, one of the main reasons why artists had headed to Rome in the first place, was highly unpopular. Thorvaldsen himself witnessed how the French stowed important pieces of art in crates in the Capitoline Museum, which he described in a letter to the Danish painter Nicolai Abildgaard in late 1797 or early 1798.[39] The Napoleonic Wars severely affected the art market in Rome since they hampered the possibilities of exporting art from Rome, particularly to Britain, where many collectors resided, which resulted in economic hardships for many artists.[40]

No known written comments on Napoleon from Thorvaldsen himself exist, but again statements from people close to Thorvaldsen can uncover some patterns of thought. Thorvaldsen's friend and benefactor Baron Herman Schubart (1756–1832) gives a highly interesting account of the sculptor's possible political antipathies concerning the Bonaparte family:

> Il me témoigna la plus grande répugnance à y aller; car bien que sculpteur il a la plus forte aversion pour la famille de Bonaparte. J'eus beau lui dire qu'un artiste ne doit pas avoir d'opinions politiques; qu'il appartient au monde entier. … Par ce préjugé politique notre bon Thorvaldsen perdit au moins 10.000 Espèces qu'il auroit facilement pu gagner.

> (He showed me the greatest repugnance to go, for although a sculptor, he has the strongest aversion for the Bonaparte family. It was no use telling him that an artist should

38 Thomasson, "Art, nationalism and politics", 166–7.

39 Bertel Thorvaldsen, "Draft of letter to Nicolai Abildgaard", Late 1797 or early 1798. m28, nr. 15, The Thorvaldsen Museum Archives, Copenhagen.

40 Wittstock, *Geschichte der Deutschen und Skandinavischen Thorwaldsen-Rezeption*, 74.

> not have political opinions, that he belongs to the whole world. … Because of this political prejudice, our good Thorvaldsen lost at least 10,000 species which he could otherwise easily have earned).[41]

The letter, written in May 1809, is revealing. Thorvaldsen's 'aversion' for the Bonaparte family became apparent to the displeased diplomat Schubart when the emperor's sister Elisa Baciocchi (1777–1820) wished to commission work from Thorvaldsen. Thorvaldsen often spent time at Schubart's country estate at Montenero in Tuscany, where Elisa requested that Thorvaldsen be sent to meet her so that she might commission some works from him. Thorvaldsen, however, returned to Rome rather than meet with Elisa, whom he apparently disliked openly.

Not only was the Danish diplomat Schubart annoyed by Thorvaldsen's lack of diplomatic tact, the letter also explicitly states that Thorvaldsen was ready to abstain from earning 10,000 species[42] because of his political disagreements with the Bonaparte family. Unlike Canova, who agreed to work for Elisa, Thorvaldsen, according to Schubart, got carried away by emotions since he politically despised the Bonaparte family and held 'political prejudices'. The tone and content of the letter reveals without a doubt that Schubart thought that it was wrong of Thorvaldsen to hold political opinions as an artist, or at least uttering them so vocally.

It is not immediately apparent why Thorvaldsen held these political prejudices against the family (who in 1809 was an ally of Thorvaldsen's native Denmark), but several explanations can be offered. One could suspect that Thorvaldsen found that Napoleon and his family had betrayed the ideals of freedom and equality originally promoted by the French Revolution. If Thorvaldsen truly supported these ideals, this might explain his unwillingness to meet with Elisa in 1809 and to work for the Bonaparte family in general. This suspicion might be reinforced by that fact that Thorvaldsen's confidante and friend Friederike Brun was close with Germaine de Staël, the woman of letters who formed an important part of the French opposition to Napoleon.

The question therefore remains why Thorvaldsen three years later would agree to execute such a formidable monument like the *Alexander Frieze* for the Quirinal Palace in Rome in Napoleon's honour shortly after his dismissal of Napoleon's sister. One explanation is rather mundane. In a letter from Karl Viktor

41 J.B. Hartmann, "Bertel Thorvaldsen Scultore Danese e i suoi soggiorni a Montenero", in *Rivista di Livorno, Rassegna di Attività Municipale a Cura del Comune vol. 5,* ed. Mostardi C. (Rome, 1958), 281.

42 One specie was the equivalent of 25 g silver, so the amount mentioned here was the equivalent of 250 kilos of silver, Editors at the Thorvaldsen Museum Archives: 'Monetary Units', arkivet.thorvaldsensmuseum.dk, 2009.

von Bonstetten (1745–1832) to Thorvaldsen's confidante Friederike Brun (1765–1835) dated 1. 1. 1812, he states that,

> In Rom darben nun drei Hundert und fünfzig Künstler; ja selbst Thorwaldsen arbeitet um geringen Preis um zu leben (In Rome three hundred and fifty artists are currently starving, yes even Thorvaldsen works at a lower price in order to survive).[43]

The prospect of a commission may have enticed Thorvaldsen into abandoning a few principles in times of economic hardship. On the other hand, the diplomat Herman Schubart and other people in Thorvaldsen's social circle may have succeeded in maturing his political views, making it apparent to him that pragmatism concerning patrons was the proper way to go for even a famous artist. Thorvaldsen may have realised that entering into an open conflict with the emperor of the French might not have seemed to be the best way forward. Or he might have thought that executing a frieze for Napoleon might be a chance to subtly utter his own views in a prominent context.

But the demise of the artwork's patron did not diminish the fame of the frieze nor of Thorvaldsen. When the Danish painter C.W. Eckersberg arrived in Rome in 1813 from Paris (where he had been a pupil of the neoclassical master Jacques-Louis David) he executed a portrait of his Roman mentor Thorvaldsen in which the *Alexander Frieze* features prominently. Eckersberg perceived the frieze to be Thorvaldsen's personal triumph.[44]

The only known description of the frieze made by Thorvaldsen doesn't reveal any political point of view.[45] The perhaps most important contemporary analysis available today is to be found in a letter from Caroline von Humboldt (1766–1829) who was married to the Prussian civil servant Wilhelm von Humboldt and was herself a shrewd art critic. It is worth noting that the Humboldt couple and Thorvaldsen had enjoyed a long and close relationship by the time Caroline wrote her letter, in fact ever since they had first met in Rome back in 1802. Apart from belonging to Thorvaldsen's inner social circle, they were in the vanguard of the German romantic movement and supported the Danish sculptor during his first years in Rome.

Caroline described the frieze to her husband as 'das Allervollkommenste, was je in neuerer Zeit ist gemacht worden' (The most perfect work made in recent times) after a visit to Thorvaldsen's studio in Rome.[46] Apart from her appreciation

43 Karl Viktor von Bonstetten, "Briefkorrespondenzen Karl Viktor von Bonstettens und seines Kreises Elfter Band 1811–1817" *1811–14 Noviziat in Hyères das Eiserne Zeitalter Neue Weltordnung*, ed. Walser-Wilhelm D. & P., (Wallstein Verlag: Göttingen, 2007), 22.

44 Christoffer Wilhelm Eckersberg, "Letter to Johann Friedrich Clemens". 11th of February 1815. Add. 301-2 (IV-50), The Manuscript Collection, Royal Library, Copenhagen.

45 Bertel Thorvaldsen, "Copy of letter to Raffaele Stern". 23rd of December 1813. m28 A I, nr. 37, The Thorvaldsen Museum Archives, Copenhagen.

46 Caroline von Humboldt, *Wilhelm und Caroline von Humboldt in ihren Briefen*, ed. Anna von

of the frieze's beauty, two of her points in this letter are of special interest. First, she describes the meeting between Alexander and the Goddess of Victory on the one hand and the Goddess of Peace on the other as 'eine so tief verstandene Gruppierung und Entgegenstellung der Figuren' (a deeply understood grouping and conflict between the figures). As such to Caroline, the frieze's most important message was not necessarily the representation of Alexander (or Napoleon's) triumphant and yet peaceful entry into a conquered city. Rather, she thought it conveyed a message of a conflict between peace and war with Alexander in an exposed position in the middle.

This contemporary understanding of the frieze's motifs adds ambiguity to the interpretations which see the frieze purely as a tribute to Napoleon. Thorvaldsen's contemporaries saw different layers in his work, including political themes. It remains, of course. her words on the frieze, but it would hardly come as a surprise if she had had the chance to discuss the matter with Thorvaldsen in person in 1817. Reflecting on the intimacy between Caroline von Humboldt and Thorvaldsen, it is tempting to consider whether her interpretation reflects Thorvaldsen's views of the frieze as well.

A second important point in the letter is Caroline von Humboldt's emphasis on the 'Greek' character of Thorvaldsen's work and how Thorvaldsen managed to produce a piece of art that surpassed that of the Greeks. In a letter dated the 22nd of June 1817, she labels the frieze 'das Schönste, was in Bildhauerei seit jener längstvergangenen großen Zeit ist gemacht worden.' ('the most beautiful thing that has been done in sculpture since the long-lost times of antiquity').[47] The identity of the sender as well as the letter's recipient should here be noted. Caroline and Wilhelm von Humboldt were, like many other German romantics, greatly preoccupied with ancient Greek art which in their world view was closely connected to politics. A good example of this view can be found in Friedrich Schiller's *Aesthetic Letters* (1794) with whom the Humboldt couple had been closely associated.[48] Through (neo)classical art, people could be cultivated and thus improve society in general. To Wilhelm von Humboldt, his wife, and their peers the artistic and political ideals of Ancient Greece therefore meant a great deal. To Humboldt, *everything* in Ancient Greece was politics including their ideals of aesthetics and art which again were closely connected with politics themselves.[49]

Sydow, bd. V; Caroline von Humboldt "Diplomatische Friedensarbeit 1815–1817", (Berlin, 1912), 320–321.

47 Humboldt, *Briefen*, 342.

48 Beiser, *Enlightenment*, 85.

49 Cord-Friedrich Berghahn, *Das Wagnis der Autonomie: Studien zu Karl Philipp Moritz, Wilhelm von Humboldt, Heinrich Gentz, Friedrich Gilly und Ludwig Tieck*, (Heidelberg, Winter Verlag, 2012), 331 and Beiser, *Enlightenment*, 111–124.

It could thus be argued that Thorvaldsen's frieze appears to the Humboldt couple as the embodiment of the romantic change in society through an aesthetic cultivation of people's minds, as well as a tribute to peace rather than to the power of Napoleon. Finally, the emphasis on the frieze's Greek character might also be interpreted as a struggle between Germanic and Latin culture. German intellectuals (including the Humboldts) increasingly saw Greek antiquity as superior to Roman antiquity, and more importantly they perceived themselves to be the true successors of ancient Greece. The French, on the contrary, were seen (and to an extent the French themselves agreed with this view) as the successors of the Roman Empire.

This view gained increasing popularity following the French invasion and subsequent occupation of the German states in 1806–7.[50] Thus an emphasis on the frieze's *Greek* character might as well be understood as an emphasis on its *Germanic* nature, and thus its superiority in a more general cultural struggle against Roman or French (Latin) art and culture. This conflict between Roman and Greek culture is examined in Suzanne L. Marchand's book *Down from Olympus* (1996). She notes that although German access to ancient Greek culture had been mediated through Latin and French authors, the German intellectuals wished to rediscover Greek culture themselves and therefore rejected 'the culture of 'Augustan' [French] Neoclassicism'.[51]

The comprehensive German understanding of politics, art, and society might be one of the reasons why German romanticism (and Thorvaldsen as well) has later come to be understood as a generally unpolitical movement, and that its rivalry with French/Latin culture came to be seen as a cultural, rather than political, struggle. The emphasis on broad education (Bildung) and its importance in shaping the minds of every citizen has led scholars to believe romanticism was unpolitical because of its focus on culture. On the contrary. It was a profoundly political movement which held the view that all societal change had to begin in the artistic and cultural sphere. Humboldt has also been perceived to have been unpolitical, partly since he argued that culture and state should be separated since he, as a liberal, didn't want the state to interfere too much in the lives of the private citizen.[52] But all of Humboldt's professional life he was deeply preoccupied with politics, and Thorvaldsen must have witnessed (and maybe par-

50 Beiser, *Enlightenment,* Arthur Lovejoy "Schiller and the Genesis of German Romanticism" in *Essays in the History of Ideas,* (Baltimore, 2019) and Johann Gottlieb Fichte, *Addresses to the German Nation*, Cambridge Texts in the History of Political Thought, ed. Gregory Moore, (New York, 2008), 57–8.

51 Marchand, *Down from Olympus,* 4.

52 Beiser, *Enlightenment,* 113–14.

ticipated too) these aesthetic, political discussions in the home of the Humboldt family who neighboured Thorvaldsen's house in Rome.[53]

In December 1816, the German philologist Friedrich von der Hagen took note of the seemingly ambiguous iconography of the *Alexanderfrieze*, while taking note of the defeated Persians' signs of 'involuntary happiness' (fig. 5) during the entry of the Macedonians. He also interprets the Persian merchants who are leaving Babylon with their goods as a 'freedom loving' people who escape the Macedonians by sailing across the Tigris River at speed. In short, he suggests, just like Caroline von Humboldt, that the motifs of the frieze aren't quite as peaceful as might be suggested after a first glance.[54]

The Danish-Norwegian priest Frederik Schmidt (1771–1840) who became friends with Thorvaldsen during his trip to Rome in 1818 describes the frieze in his diary on the 11th of October 1818. He notes that 'Babylons Commandant M med sine Børn af forskjellig Alder yttrende meer eller mindre Frygt' (the children of Babylon's commander M. show various degrees of fear).[55] This view, of course, collides with the intention of showing Alexander entering a city whose population welcomes him and shows trust. Contemporaries thus identified conflicting messages when seeing the defeated Mazaeus' children meeting the victorious Alexander.

In March 1818, the Swedish author Per Atterbom made a description of the frieze which presents another interesting view of the messages in the artwork. The description was later translated and published in a magazine to the Danish public. Atterbom regretted that Napoleon 'neglected to see the perhaps only truly beautiful aesthetic tribute which was ever made in his honour'. Atterbom, however, was not convinced whether the frieze was truly a tribute to Napoleon:

> Jeg lader det iøvrigt staae ved sit Værd, i hvorvidt han vilde føle sig smigret derved, naar han havde bemærket de Venner af Friheden, der af alle Kræfter roe bort over Tigris, og om han havde forstaaet dette snue Vink om det Frivillige i Babyloniernes Glæde?
>
> (I will leave it to be seen, whether or not he [Napoleon] would have felt flattered by it, had he noticed those friends of liberty who where rowing away with all their might across the Tigris, and whether or not he would have understood this shrewd hint to the true nature of the voluntarity of the Babylonians joy.).[56]

53 Thiele II, 86.

54 Friedrich Heinrich von der Hagen, 1780–1856: *Briefe in die Heimat aus Deutschland, der Schweiz und Italien*, vol. 2, (Berlin: Josef Max & Comp., 1821), 335.

55 Frederik Schmidt, *Provst Frederik Schmidts dagbøger*, vol. 1–2, eds. Ole Jacobsen og Johanne Brandt-Nielsen, (København: Gads Forlag, 1966–69), vol. 2, 384–385.

56 Per Atterbom, "Printed Danish translation of letter to Erik Gustaf Geijer," 16th of June 1821. Småtryk-Samling 1821, The Thorvaldsen Museum Archives, Copenhagen.

Atterbom, like Friedrich von der Hagen, thought that the merchants depicted on the frieze were fleeing the invading Macedonian army. He thus interprets the frieze to contain subterfuge criticism of emperor Napoleon a provocative claim, considering that Napoleon originally commissioned the work.

Atterbom's view has since become controversial among scholars, who have tended to discard his argument. Atterbom has been described as politically naive, and that he 'wanted the frieze to be critical of Napoleon'.[57] This might be, but Atterbom was nevertheless quite close with Thorvaldsen as were several other people behind remarks that point towards ambiguous motifs in Thorvaldsen's *Alexander Frieze.* Indeed, whether Atterbom was politically naive or not, isn't really the issue. He disseminates a view of the frieze which has hardly been taken seriously ever since by scholars. By proposing the quite direct view that the frieze was no tribute to Napoleon, he indirectly expands on Humboldt's more subtle analysis.

Atterbom's claim is somewhat strengthened by Thiele. Even Thorvaldsen's cautious biographer, who was most reluctant to ascribe political opinions to Thorvaldsen, mentioned that he had heard, by hearsay in Rome, that a fisher depicted on the frieze shared facial features with the French emperor:

> Angaaende denne Fisker, da er det i Rom fortalt, at Kunstneren, ved i Quirinalexemplaret at modellere hans Hoved, skal have tænkt paa Portraitet af Frankrigs Keiser, som paa den Tid var en verdslig Modsætning af Fiskeren Petrus, hvis Plads han i Rom havde indtaget.
>
> (As for this fisherman, it is said in Rome that the artist, in modelling his head in the Quirinal copy, should have had in mind the portrait of the Emperor of France, who at that time was a secular opposite of Peter the fisherman, whose place he had taken in Rome.).[58]

Thiele adds that he does not guarantee the truth in this anecdote, but that 'it might have suited Thorvaldsen's sarcastic caprice'. Not only is Thiele's remark of interest – the way he formulates it is too. Thiele served an absolutist state when he wrote the biography in 1831. This might explain Thiele's cautious way of expressing himself regarding a sensitive topic. For an audience more used to living with censorship, this may very well have been a direct way of stating that the message of the frieze was double edged, and that Thorvaldsen deliberately made it possible for viewers to conclude differently depending on their political standpoint.

57 Thomasson, "Art, nationalism", 172.
58 Just Mathias Thiele, *1831,* 126.

The *Alexander Frieze* and the Public Sphere

Most spectators would probably not have seen the frieze 'in situ' in the Quirinal Palace. Rather it would have been more likely for visitors in Rome to see the version of the frieze which was found in Thorvaldsen's studio in Rome, like Caroline von Humboldt, Per Atterbom and Mendelssohn did. This might have affected peoples' perception of the frieze. Did Thorvaldsen or his assistants for instance provide visitors with suggestions as to how the frieze should be interpreted? Thorvaldsen's studio became something of a tourist attraction, where even Pope Leo XII would visit in 1826.

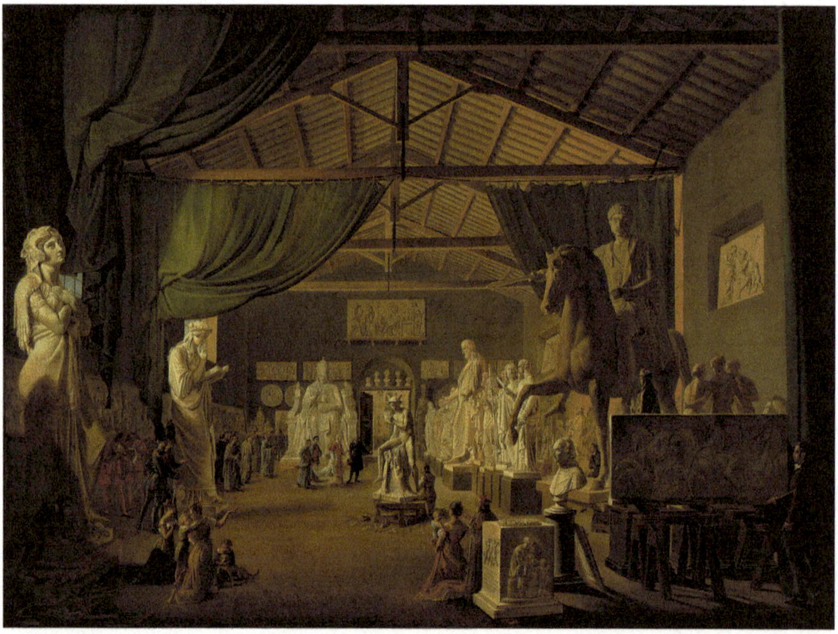

Figure 9. Ditlev Martens, *Pope Leo XII Visiting Thorvaldsen's Studios in the Piazza Barberini, 18 October 1826*, The National Gallery of Denmark, Copenhagen.

It is unknown how many people visited the Quirinal Palace and saw the frieze there. A great many people would have seen reproductions in newspapers or when visiting private homes decorated with either plaster or terracotta copies of the frieze. Thorvaldsen himself commissioned the Swiss copper engraver Samuel Amsler to publish a copper engraving of the *Alexander Frieze* in 1835 after drawings made by the German painter Johann Friedrich Overbeck.[59] In general

59 *Kjøbenhavnsposten,* 20th of February. Thorvaldsens Museums Småtryk-Samling 1836, The Thorvaldsen Museum Archives, Copenhagen.

the 'targeted' audience seems to have been the educated public who subscribed to journals, travelled to some extent, and had rudimentary knowledge of art, history, and literature.[60]

Thorvaldsen as Alexander

The Danish historian Christian Molbech notes in 1820 during a visit to Rome that the frieze had become 'Thorvaldsen's triumph' regarding the Dane's rivalry with the Italian Canova.[61] These conflicting views of 'Germanic' vs 'Latin' art signified more than just aesthetic preferences. From a Danish perspective it marked the beginning of a nationalistic view of Thorvaldsen. Thorvaldsen's genius originated from his Danish upbringing according to Molbech. The German composer Mendelssohn had praised Thorvaldsen as the foremost of the 'German' artists alongside Beethoven and Goethe in 1831 and after seeing the *Alexander Frieze* he noted:

> Vom Alexanderszug müßt ich einmal einen ganzen Brief schreiben; denn solchen Eindruck hat mir die Skulptur noch gar nicht gemacht, wie da. Ich gehe alle Woche hin, und sehe mir nur das an, und ziehe mit ein in Babylon.
>
> (I ought to write an entire letter on Alexander's entry [into Babylon] since no other sculpture has ever made such an impression on me like that one. I go there every week to see only that and follow the procession into Babylon myself).[62]

Thorvaldsen and his frieze, in the eyes of Germans and Scandinavians, thus became a counterweight to the otherwise cultural dominance of Italy and France, which is supported by later dismissive French views of Thorvaldsen and his art.[63]

It also became a rather popular view to see the frieze as either Thorvaldsen's or art's triumph in general rather than stress the artwork's association with Napoleon or the Danish monarch. This view became explicit when Thorvaldsen returned to his native Copenhagen after more than forty years in Rome. The famous Danish poet Hans Christian Andersen wrote a poem in honour of Thorvaldsen and his *Alexander Frieze* on that occasion, celebrating Thorvaldsen as an Alexander figure.[64] Indeed the newspapers were flooded with comparisons

60 Hauser, 57–8 & Busk-Jepsen, K.: 'Caffè Greco: Art Temple, Post Office and Cosmopolitan Sanctuary', arkivet.thorvaldsensmuseum.dk, 2014.

61 Molbech, C.: *Reise giennem en Deel af Tyskland, Frankrige, England og Italien i Aarene 1819 og 1820 vol. 3,* (København, 1822), 206–209 and 221–229.

62 Felix Mendelssohn Bartholdy, *Reisebriefe von Felix Mendelssohn Bartholdy aus den Jahren 1830 bis 1832.* Paul Mendelssohn Bartholdy (ed.), (Leipzig, Drei Brücken Verlag, 1861) 113.

63 d'Angers, "Lettre sur Thorwaldsen".

64 Hans Christian Andersen, "Poem to Bertel Thorvaldsen", 7th of October 1838. m33, nr. 16. The Thorvaldsen Museum Archives, Copenhagen.

between Thorvaldsen and Alexander and the frieze as a symbol of the triumph of art in society in those days.[65]

The only negative criticism that the *Alexander Frieze* received from Scandinavian and German viewers, concerned the figure of Alexander himself on the frieze. The anonymous author of an article in the German newspaper from 1827 "Literarische Blätter der Börsen-Halle" finds that the figure of Alexander is a clear exception from the other depicted on the frieze who reflect 'the Etruscan calmness':

> bei den Begriffen, die wir von diesem Karl XII. der alten Welt haben, können wir nicht umhin, ihm eine minder studierte Haltung zu wünschen; er hat die Welt erobert, aber er ist zu voll von seinem Triumph; er muß mehr Stolz und minder Eitelkeit gehabt haben.
>
> (By the notions we have of this Charles XII of the ancient world, we couldn't have failed to wish to see him in a more rehearsed posture. He has conquered the world, but he is too full of his own triumph, he should have shown more pride and less vanity).[66]

The author of this text is clearly opposed to Alexander and to violence in general, comparing him to the brutal Swedish warrior king Charles XII (1682–1718) whose campaigns had laid waste to Sweden and large tracts of Eastern Europe. He is not impressed by military glory which in a way reflects Caroline von Humboldt's interpretation of the frieze from 1817.

This view is again expressed in 1830 in the newspaper "Das Inland" in which Alexander's posture is criticised not only for his exaggerated vanity but also for having too close a resemblance with Canova.[67] In 1839 in the literary magazine "Kunst-Blatt" the critique is even heavier, and again the figure of Alexander bears the brunt of the criticism being labelled a 'theatre caricature'.[68] Alexander was clearly no popular figure around this time.

In 1843, a year before Thorvaldsen's death, an article on the *Alexander Frieze* in "Conversationslexikon für Bildende Kunst" reveals to which degree the views of Caroline von Humboldt and Per Atterbom lived on in the later reception history of the frieze. Apart from generally praising the frieze as an important piece of art, descriptions of the frieze's fisherman with Napoleon's facial features as reference to Napoleon seizing the pope's palace, the frightened children and Persian

---

65 *Kjøbenhavnsposten,* 8th of October. Thorvaldsens Museums Småtryk-Samling 1838, The Thorvaldsen Museum Archives, Copenhagen.

66 *'Literarische Blätter der Börsen-Halle'.* "Thorwaldsen's Werkstatt zu Rom". Thorvaldsens Museums Småtryk-Samling M17,13, The Thorvaldsen Museum Archives, Copenhagen.

67 *Das Inland,* Thorvaldsens Museums Småtryk-Samling M17,20, The Thorvaldsen Museum Archives, Copenhagen.

68 *Kunst-Blatt Gebildete Stände*, No. 18, 1839, 70–71, Heidelberg, Heidelberg Universitätsbibliothek.

merchants fleeing Alexander are all to be found.[69] Additionally, the figure of Alexander, the symbol of power and war, is increasingly ridiculed by contemporaries. This description in a contemporary encyclopaedic article would generally give a good picture of the authoritative view of the frieze at the time.

This view is amplified in 1846 in "Illustrierte Zeitung" where Thorvaldsen is even compared to Ludwig van Beethoven who famously removed the dedication to Napoleon in his *Eroica Symphony,* since Thorvaldsen, according to the anonymous author, like Beethoven refused to pay tribute to Napoleon with the frieze.[70] Beethoven's rejection of Napoleon's regime after the composer's initial enthusiasm is one of the most famous political statements made by an artist during the Napoleonic era. For Thorvaldsen's *Alexander Frieze* to be compared with Beethoven's *Eroica Symphony* is a testimony to the fact that the view of the *Alexander Frieze* as a monument critical of Napoleon was firmly established.

Rather than supporting the French emperor, signs of protest were found in the frieze. It is perhaps in this light that Thorvaldsen's only other work depicting Alexander the Great should be viewed: The already mentioned plaster relief from 1832 commissioned by the Bavarian king Ludwig I which portrays a drunk Alexander burning down the Persian ceremonial capital of Persepolis much to the despair of the horrified Persians. It shows another more violent and sinister side of Napoleon's alter ego, a side which most art critics were acutely aware of in the 19th century. The frieze's commissioning shortly after the second French Revolution of 1830 might reflect the conservative values of the political reaction of the period. The Bavarian king, sceptical of the universal monarchy, wished to emphasise the destructiveness of military 'glories' of the universal monarchies of Alexander and Napoleon. And, while Thorvaldsen supplied him with the frieze, the sculptor himself had an opportunity to add a last comment to his most renowned monument.

Conclusion

Studies of the primary source material at hand reveal that Bertel Thorvaldsen held political opinions which were often critical of monarchy and authoritarian power, even though written statements from his own hand are rare. I argue that he held critical views of the Bonaparte family, as revealed in Schubart's letter of 1809. Analyses made by people who knew Thorvaldsen well, such as Caroline

69 *Conversationslexikon für Bildende Kunst*, M17,49, Thorvaldsens Museums Småtryk-Samling 1843, The Thorvaldsen Museum Archives, Copenhagen.

70 *Illustrirte Zeitung*, VII, no. 167, Thorvaldsens Museums Småtryk-Samling 1846, The Thorvaldsen Museum Archives, Copenhagen.

von Humboldt and Per Atterbom, reveal that they interpreted the meaning of the *Alexander Frieze* to be ambiguous, suggesting that a conflict is apparent in the frieze next to its motifs of peace and tribute to Alexander. Unlike earlier scholarship, I consider it highly likely that Thorvaldsen ensured, on purpose, that the frieze could be interpreted both as a tribute to Napoleon as well as a critique of him and his policies. This subtlety ensured that the frieze could be installed in the first place as well as guaranteeing the frieze's artistic and political relevance in the aftermath of the emperor's fall from grace.

The French emperor appears to have held a positive view of the artwork (although he never saw it *in situ*), and the German opposition to the French regarded the frieze as highly critical of Napoleon. As such Thorvaldsen managed to cater to both the feelings of a ruling prince as well as the political opposition of the German romantic bourgeoisie. Thorvaldsen had the resources to show political agency as an artist but was forced to do it in a subtle way, otherwise his work would be censored, hence the ambiguity of many of his works including the *Alexander Frieze*. The story behind the commissioning of the *Alexander Frieze* is a fine example of his artistic agency. In a sense Thorvaldsen succeeded in being both an idealistic artist and a shrewd diplomat as well as an efficient businessman, ensuring the popularity of his own artwork despite the highly volatile political landscape. The frieze thus became a triumph for Thorvaldsen's quest for artistic independence.

Moreover, as already demonstrated, it is beyond any doubt when reviewing the frieze's reception history in the latter decades of the 19th century, that many observers continued to interpret the frieze either as a critique of Napoleon and war, as art's triumph over politics, or as artistic proof of the romantic German culture's superiority over Latin culture, thus making the *Alexander Frieze* part of the nascent nationalistic conflicts in Europe. In this way the commissioning, execution, display, and reception history of the frieze reflect the political and societal change the European continent underwent in the decades between the revolutions of 1789 and 1848. Artists such as Thorvaldsen found themselves in the middle of a political conflict between princely rule and bourgeois dreams of free constitutions, and this was reflected in the artwork of the era.

As examined in the introduction, several factors such as a modernist, one-sided interpretation of neoclassicism in general, Thorvaldsen's role as a national icon in Denmark and the conflicted view of political romanticism in Germany can help explain why the analysis of Thorvaldsen's art in a political context has been underappreciated by scholarship in much of the 20th century. It reveals to us how difficult it is to analyse and understand political communication and political opinions in a society which was characterised by authoritarian rule, censorship, and political attempts to change this condition. In early 19th-century Europe, art was aptly used as a means of political communication by various factions. For posterity, it is thus immensely useful as historical source material. Thorvaldsen's *Alexander Frieze* is a poignant example of this, and his art, as well as the general artistic output of the period, deserves to be further examined in the future.

About the Authors

Inga Kapustian is a guest researcher at the University of Southern Denmark's Hans Christian Andersen Center. She attained her PhD degree with the thesis about lifelong learning education in Sweden at the Institute of Information Technologies and Learning Tools of the National Academy of Science in Ukraine (2012). She has worked as an Associate Professor at Ukraine's Poltava National Pedagogical University and the Odesa International Humanitarian University at the departments of Foreign Language and Literature. Her research interests include Scandinavian and Slavic literatures.

The Hans Christian Andersen Centre
Department of the Study of Culture
The University of Southern Denmark
ingaka@sdu.dk

Lea Grosen Jørgensen has a PhD in Comparative Literature from Aarhus University. Her dissertation focused on the reception of Old Norse literature in the writings of Adam Oehlenschläger and N. F. S. Grundtvig. She has taught courses about romantic and modern medievalism and co-written the anthology Middelalderisme i dansk romantisk litteratur (Aarhus University Press 2023).

leagj92@msn.com

Anders Kristian Strand is Associate Professor of Comparative Literature at the University of Bergen. He obtained his doctoral degree with a thesis on linguistic thinking in translations by Rilke and George. Much of his research has since focused on modernist literature and aesthetic theory. He is currently completing a book on river poetry from Ausonius to our time and another on the idea of decay in the interwar period. Since 2014 he has been co-editor of Norsk Litteraturvitenskapelig Tidsskrift.

Department of Linguistic, Literary and Aesthetic Studies
University of Bergen
anders.strand@uib.no

Edward Payne is an Assistant Professor in Art History at Aarhus University. Specializing in the Mediterranean Baroque, his research engages with topics including violence, skin, sensory perception, caricature, and ugliness. He has organized several exhibitions, notably *Visions and Nightmares: Four Centuries of Spanish Drawings* (Morgan Library & Museum, 2014); *Between Heaven and Hell: The Drawings of Jusepe de Ribera* (Meadows Museum, 2017); and *Ribera: Art of Violence* (Dulwich Picture Gallery, 2018–19). Edward has held research fellowships at the British School at Rome (2009) and the Clark Art Institute (2021).

Department of Art History, Aesthetics & Culture and Museology
Aarhus University
Co-director: Center for Early Modern Studies
edward.payne@cc.au.dk

Hans Erik Havsteen holds a master's degree from the University of Oxford and a BA in history from the University of Copenhagen. He has previously worked as an assistant at the Thorvaldsen Museum Archives, as editor of Politiken Historie and as host at the podcast 'Kongerækken'. He is currently working as an editor in publishing alongside finishing his master's degree in history and art history at the University of Copenhagen.

he.hav@hotmail.com